D1526238

Owning and Using Scholarship:
An IP Handbook for Teachers and Researchers

Kevin L. Smith, JD

Thank you, Deborah, for all your support, for this project and for all my endeavors at Duke.

K

Association of College and Research Libraries
A division of the American Library Association
Chicago, Illinois 2014

The paper used in this publication meets the minimum requirements of American National Standard for Information Sciences–
Permanence of Paper for Printed Library Materials, ANSI Z39.48-
1992. ∞

Library of Congress Cataloging-in-Publication Data

Smith, Kevin L. (Kevin Lindsay), 1959- author.
  Owning and using scholarship : an IP handbook for teachers and
researchers / Kevin L. Smith, JD.
     pages cm
  Includes bibliographical references and index.
  ISBN 978-0-8389-8747-6 (pbk. : alk. paper) 1. Intellectual
property--United States. 2. Copyright--United States. 3. Fair
use (Copyright)--United States. 4. License agreements--United
States. 5. Learning and scholarship--United States. 6. Commu-
nication in learning and scholarship--United States. 7. Research-
-Technological innovations. 8. Creation (Literary, artistic, etc.)-
-Research. I. Title.
  KF2994.S63 2014
  346.7304'8--dc23
                          2014041050

Printed in the United States of America.

18 17 16 15 14 5 4 3 2 1

Contents

This book is dedicated with
fondness and respect to the
memory of my father,

Lindsay Gordon Smith,

who taught me both the rigors
and the joys of scholarship and
research.

Technology and the Growing Problem of Intellectual Property in Academia

SCHOLARS HAVE always been plagued by an ambivalent attitude toward intellectual property, as the following simple story demonstrates. According to the legend of Saint Columba, who became the first abbot of the monastery at Iona and died in 597 CE, the famous Irish saint was involved in what may have been the world's first conflict over academic copyrights. As *Butler's Lives of the Saints* (1956, 507) notes, "Like the true scholar he was, Columba dearly loved books and spared no pains to obtain them." The result of this passion was the making of a surreptitious copy of a psalter in the possession of Columba's former master, Finnian. When Finnian learned of the copy, which rendered his own possession no longer exclusive in the land of Ireland, he objected bitterly. The dispute over who should own the copy escalated and eventually reached King Diarmaid, who rendered the first, and probably most cryptic, copyright verdict in recorded history. Diarmaid's ruling, "As the calf belongs to the cow, so the copy belongs to the book,"[1] awarded the unauthorized copy to Finnian and led to even greater conflict.

Several aspects of this story from the sixth century make it particularly relevant to a discussion of intellectual property for twenty-first-century academics. First, of course, is the fact that both of the contestants for ownership of the disputed book were scholars. The tension, for scholars, between the desire to assert ownership over ideas and their expression and the need to disseminate those ideas as widely as possible in order to encourage learning and increase academic standing has existed for a very long time. And, of course, scholars are today, as they were in Columba's time, both creators and consumers of intellectual property, a circumstance that does much to explain the persistent sense of ambivalence about copyrights. It is worth pointing out that Columba's copying did not deprive Finnian of the valuable manuscript he had obtained. The "non-exclusive" nature of intellectual property remains a fundamental problem for copyright regulation in particular.

Second, we should note that neither Finnian nor Columba had much in the way of economic incentive; their conflict was about reputation more than money. When the modern forerunners of copyright law developed in the seventeenth century, they were always primarily aimed at creating economic incentives, which is one reason they have never fit comfortably with the needs and concerns of scholars.[2] As copyright scholar William Patry (2009) notes, these economic incentives work best when consumers set the value for intellectual content and creators benefit directly from that value exchange. For academics, however, publishing intermediaries both set the value for scholarly works and collect all the profits, so there is a fundamental failure in the incentive structure.

Finally, there is a modern ring to the realization that the legal ruling intended to settle this dispute did no such thing; ultimately (and

---

1. The wording of the verdict varies slightly in different sources. This particular version is taken from the modern retelling of this "well-attested" legend by James J. O'Donnell (1998, 92).

2. For the origins of modern copyright law, see Patterson 1968 and Rose 1993.

for reasons more complex than just a dispute over rights to a copy of the psalms), Columba's clan fought a short war with the followers of Diarmaid, which led directly to Columba's exile and settlement of Iona (see Butler 1956, 508). For us, the point is that, even fifteen centuries ago, legal rules based on analogies with personal or real property (like a cow!) seemed ill-suited to settle the disputes that arise over intellectual property, especially among academics. As we shall see, this "property" language has always been problematic and is especially ill-suited for thinking about IP in the age of the Internet (see Patry 2009, 109–31).

The regulation of intellectual property has obviously come a long way since King Diarmaid issued his decision. The last twenty years, however, have seen two particularly dramatic changes, one in copyright law itself and one in the conditions that obtain for the production and dissemination of scholarship, that have fundamentally altered the IP landscape for scholarship.[3]

A REVOLUTION IN COPYRIGHT LAW

For the first two hundred years of copyright law in the United States, it was necessary to take some action in order to obtain protection for a work. Under the first copyright law passed in the United States, the Copyright Act of 1790 (1 Stat. 124), protection was available only for books, charts, and maps that were printed and sold, and it was extended only after a copy of the published material was deposited with the clerk of the local district court.[4] When the law was completely revamped in 1909, a much broader range of material could be protected by copyright,

---

3. As will be explained in chapter 2, *intellectual property*, or *IP*, refers to several quite different types of regulation over the productions of authorship and invention. Copyright is one type of IP regulation.

4. The full text of the Copyright Act of 1790, which is only two pages long, can be found on the website of the US Copyright Office at www.copyright.gov/history/1790act.pdf.

and the scope of that protection was expanded considerably. At the same time, the familiar requirement that a work carry the © symbol was added. From 1909 until 1989, works were entitled to federal copyright protection only if they were published with notice, which was usually provided by that well-known symbol.[5]

This situation began to change in 1988,[6] when the United States finally joined the Berne Convention for the Protection of Literary and Artistic Works after resisting that international agreement for over one hundred years.[7] One of the requirements imposed on all signers of the Berne Convention is that the "enjoyment and exercise" of the rights outlined may not be made conditional on any "formalities," such as notice, registration, or deposit (see Berne Convention 1971, art 5(2)). As part of compliance with these new obligations, the United States began dismantling its formalities with the Berne Convention Implementation Act of 1988, which amended the 1976 Copyright Act.[8] The abolition of the last of the copyright formalities was completed in 1992, and from thence forward, copyright protection became automatic.[9] It is now the case that copyright protection adheres in any original work from the moment that it is fixed in tangible form.

---

5. The text of the 1909 Copyright Act is also available from the US Copyright Office, at www.copyright.gov/history/1909act.pdf.

6. The transition to the type of regime required by international copyright regimes really began with the adoption of the Copyright Act of 1976.

7. The Berne Convention was first adopted, primarily by European countries, in 1886. At that time, the US publishing industry relied heavily on producing cheap editions of English books and did not want the United States to agree to a treaty that required mutual recognition of copyright laws between nations. Now, ironically, the United States has become a strong proponent of increasingly strict copyright enforcement across borders in spite of being such a latecomer to the agreement.

8. The Implementation Act is Pub. L. No. 100-568, 102 Stat. 2853 (1988). The full text of 1976 Copyright Act, which took effect on January 1, 1978, and is still in force, can be found at www.copyright.gov/title17. The copyright law is Title 17 of the United States Code.

9. See Patry 2009, 67. The final amendment to the Copyright Act removing formalities was the Copyright Amendments Act of 1992, Pub. L. No. 102-307, 106 Stat. 264 (1992).

Although hardly the sort of event that captures the public imagination, this shift to automatic protection really was revolutionary for American copyright law. Even twenty years after this change, many people still do not realize that they own copyrights. Yet every time that anybody records an original work—and as we shall see, the standard of originality is very low—that person owns a copyright. This means that notes for a lecture, an e-mail or letter to Aunt Jane, a tourist's photograph, or even a list of things to do on a Saturday afternoon now gives rise to copyright protection (although many of those rights would never be asserted). From a situation where one had to take a concrete action in order to obtain a copyright, we have now moved to one where nearly everyone holds these rights, usually unawares.

I often begin copyright presentations by asking my audience who among them owns a copyright. Usually only a few hands are raised initially, even when the audience is mostly academics. As I explain this change in our copyright law, a few more hands tentatively go up. It is truly amazing how hard it is to get every hand raised, as some people continue to resist the idea that they own a copyright in every original work they create. Copyright is often believed to be rare and difficult to obtain, although the truth is exactly opposite. This difference between copyright and other types of intellectual property will be explored in the next chapter.

For scholars and academics, this revolution means that both the inputs of their research and the outputs they create are protected by the exclusive rights granted by copyright law. For academic authors of an older generation, this is a genuine surprise since the conditions were very different when they began their careers. In those days, since copyright came into play only when a work was published with notice, academics seldom owned the rights at all; the rights were created by publication and held from the start by publishers. Today, academics hold exclusive rights of reproduction, distribution, public performance, display, and creation of derivative works in everything they write. Publishers obtain those rights only if the original author or creator transfers them, either by license or by a contract of assignment.[10] Even scholars who came to scholarship more recently sometimes struggle to grasp the notion that they own a valuable and protectable asset as soon as they fix original scholarly works.

The positive aspect of this change to automatic protection, then, is precisely that scholars *do* now own copyright in all of their works and are in a better position than ever before to negotiate over the exercise of those rights in ways that will benefit them personally and professionally. But there is also a significant downside to this revolution; it has resulted in virtually zero growth in the US public domain over the past two decades. Works that were already published and protected by copyright when the law changed will remain protected until at least 2018 (except for works protected before 1963 for which the copyright was not renewed), while works created after the new copyright law was passed will not enter the public domain until 2047 at the earliest.[11] Virtually nothing created in the current generation will become public property during our lifetimes.[12]

In previous years, it was possible to place a work into the public domain simply by distributing it without a copyright notice; the formalities required by law facilitated voluntary sharing. With the change to automatic protection, it became much harder for a creator to share her work free of the restrictions now mandated by copyright law. Professor James Boyle (2008, 45), in his book *The Public Domain*, calls this "a second enclosure movement" and draws an explicit analogy with the efforts almost four hundred years ago to enclose public land in England for the

---

10. Throughout this book I will say "author" and "write" when I really mean the whole variety of ways in which copyrightable subject matter is created—by writing, photography, audio or video recording, digital means of all sorts, and even by building a structure. This usage can be attributed to ease of expression or to the limited experiences of an old-fashioned author, but it should always be understood to encompass the variety of creation that copyright itself embraces.

11. The terms of protection of the Copyright Act, Title 17 of the United States Code, are detailed in chapter 3. A useful chart for determining the length of protection for a particular work, which can be extremely complex, is Hirtle 2014.

12. One exception to the general rule that no US publications are entering the public domain is works created by the federal government, which are excepted from copyright protection by 17 U.S.C. § 105.

benefit of private interests. Although it is still possible, using mechanisms like the Creative Commons licensing scheme that let authors give prior permission for certain uses, to dedicate a work to the public,[13] the default position for work released without intentional reservation of rights has changed dramatically, from free for use to protected virtually forever. Indeed, Professor Boyle (2008, 184) goes so far as to suggest that the ideal solution to this "enclosure" problem would be a return to a simple and minimalist set of copyright formalities.

It is supremely ironic that this change in the default legal position toward "unintentional" copyright protection occurred just as the Internet, an immense tool for sharing creative and scholarly work, along with lots and lots of junk, was being developed. The impact of the Internet on university campuses, and on scholarship in general, has been tremendous, but that impact has been limited by the fact that nearly everything we find online is subject to copyright protection. It is true that courts have acknowledged an "implied license" when an author posts material to the Web that allows users to read those pages and to make the ephemeral copies in their computer's memory that are necessary for viewing (see, e.g., Field v. Google Inc., 412 F. Supp. 2d 1106 (D. Nev. 2006)). Beyond the scope of this implied license, however, the default assumption must be that what we find on the Internet is not available for us to use, share, or rework without explicit permission. This means that lots of material that we could use for teaching or scholarship is more ready to hand than ever before, but also more likely to be locked up by copyright rules. Indeed, the situation is even worse when we fully understand the way copyright protections apply to the new digital technologies, a subject to which we now turn.

---

13. See http://creativecommons.org. The Creative Commons licensing scheme will be discussed in detail in chapter 6.

THE DIGITAL REVOLUTION

It is hardly necessary to describe the dramatic changes wrought in entertainment, communication, and social life by the rapid growth of the Internet and digital technologies; these changes are well known and have been effectively described elsewhere.[14] The standard practices of scholars have also changed dramatically, of course. It is becoming hard now to recall how scholarship was practiced in the age of typewriters and before the ubiquitous communication enabled by cell phones and e-mail. But it remains important to dissect some of the changes that the digital revolution has brought to scholarly practice and to consider what those changes mean from the perspective of intellectual property rights.

First, as has already been suggested, the Internet has given scholars an unprecedented access to the "inputs" of scholarship; the journal articles, bibliographic references, images, video, and music upon which scholars build are all available at the touch of a button. Searches that would have required endless flipping through a card catalog or print index in the past now are accomplished at the touch of a computer key, either using a library's online catalog and licensed databases or relying on the mysterious algorithms that drive Google Scholar. Whereas in previous years most research time was spent locating exactly the right materials for a new work, now the process of location is relatively trivial. Selection of the best sources from among the mass of material that is found so easily is where most time must be invested. And once materials are located and chosen for a new project, scholars have the added burden of knowing just what one can use and which uses are permitted under copyright law or based on the license agreement that permits access.[15]

---

14. Even a long list of titles discussing the changes wrought in the Internet age would have to be highly selective and idiosyncratic. My relatively short list would include Barbrook 2007; Barnet 2004; Benkler 2006; Friedman 2005; Palfrey 2008; and Sunstein 2007. Even more idiosyncratically, I might add Brand 1999.

15. Internet access to many materials requires users to agree to sometimes quite elaborate licensing terms. Sometimes individual users "click through" these terms on a particular website and create binding obligations without realizing it. For many of

In a speech given to the higher education group EDUCAUSE in November 2009, Harvard law professor Lawrence Lessig vividly described the changed situation for academics as they go about using the inputs that are now so readily available:

> If copyright law, at its core, regulates something called
> "copies," then in an analog world … many uses of culture
> were copyright-free. They didn't trigger copyright law,
> because no copy was made. But in the digital world, very
> few uses are copyright free because in a digital world …
> all uses produce a copy. (quoted in Kolowich 2009)

As Lessig indicates, the Internet, which facilitates so much access to the material scholars need, is, in a sense, one giant copy machine. Every access to a web page creates a copy of the content of that page in the memory of a computer or mobile device. Using a printed copy of a book or article raised no copyright issues at all, once that material was legally purchased by the scholar or borrowed from a library. The short quotations that would be incorporated in a new work of scholarship were the quintessential instance of "fair use," about which we will have much more to say. But in the digital world, multiple copies of entire works—journal articles, film, music, and images—are routinely transferred from computer to computer, sometimes without the awareness of the user, and the new possibilities for creative reuse, especially for purposes of detailed criticism or analysis, stretch the boundaries of fair use. Scholarship has thus become contested in a way it never was in the past, because putatively unauthorized copies, much like Columba's psalter, abound on the digital desktops of scholars around the world.

---

the most important scholarly resources, however, access is purchased by institutions, usually through their libraries. Access to these resources is often very expensive and subject to significant restriction. Because scholars who work for these universities usually have immediate and unfettered access to these databases, they sometimes do not realize the impact of the costs or the licensing process.

In addition to greater access to scholarly materials and greater conflicts over their use, the Internet has fostered other dramatic changes in the practice of scholarship. One is the growth of informal channels of scholarly communications. A great deal of scholarly dialogue is carried out over e-mail today, and "real-time" forms of communication like Twitter are showing up on the academic horizon as well. At Duke University, students in an introductory film class recently engaged in a "Twitter Film Festival" for a final project, spending an entire day watching films and sharing their thoughts and reviews with anyone following their feed using the social networking service (see Read 2009). If this seems like a clever aberration today, we should remember that much of the technology we now take for granted did a few years ago as well.

One technology that is catching on rapidly, at least in some disciplines, is blogging. In legal scholarship, for example, blogs have become an important vehicle for conversation and for sharing nascent ideas and even portions of works that will later be published in a more traditional fashion.[16] So important have legal blogs become that one scholar has been tracking the citation of blogs in judicial opinions, which is, of course, the pinnacle of scholarly respectability for the field (Peoples 2009). The use of blogs may be more readily acceptable in law, where the system of student-edited law reviews has led to a long tradition of informal, presubmission peer review for legal articles. Nevertheless, other fields are beginning to use blogs in similar ways as collaborative spaces for active scholarly reflection; the *Savage Minds* blog in anthropology (http://savageminds.org) is one highly influential example. In mathematics, blogs can be used to harness the talents of researchers around the globe to solve seemingly intractable problems. The Polymath project, where a mathematician who posts high-level mathematical problems to a blog is finding that they

---

16. Two of the most influential legal blogs are *The Volokh Conspiracy* (www.washingtonpost.com/news/volokh-conspiracy) and *Balkinization* (http://balkin.blogspot.com). Both are collaborative works by groups of scholars and frequently feature prepublication release of book and article ideas, as well as very high-quality post-publication reviews.

are often solved very quickly, is a powerful example of this radical new approach to collaborative scholarship (Rehmeyer 2009).

Many universities are deploying system-wide, multiuser blogging technologies, clearly expecting that this will become a heavily adopted technology for classes and for research. The potential benefits for field research, where scholars at great distance from each other can jointly craft a report or article with unaccustomed ease, is another example of why blogs (or something like them) are likely to become a fixture in scholarly work.

Another change in scholarly practice that has been facilitated by digital technologies is the ability to incorporate various types of media into a scholarly argument and to build works of scholarship that are wholly digital. For a music professor or a scholar of film studies, there is no longer any reason, other than potential copyright restrictions, to write about a symphony or a movie without actually allowing readers to see or hear what is being discussed.[17] Indeed, the film studies professor can now create her study of a particular theme or technique entirely as a film, weaving clips from various examples into a unique visual narrative. As we will see later, there is real debate about whether this kind of activity should be permitted based on current copyright laws, but there is no doubt that digital technologies offer wonderful opportunities for creative teaching as well as scholarship.

In addition to the chance to create traditional forms in new media, it is also possible now to approach certain types of research in wholly new ways. For example, data sets can now be turned into digital visualizations that can provide new perspectives[18] and even, as in the case of brain mapping, allow researchers to see something that would otherwise be invisible

---

17. In *Art History and Its Publications in the Electronic Age,* Hilary Ballon and Mariet Westermann (2006) make much the same point regarding scholarship in art history.

18. An IBM research group is now offering a free data visualization service called Many Eyes (http://www-958.ibm.com/software/analytics/manyeyes) that exemplifies the possibilities for even relatively unsophisticated users to exploit digital technology in order to present research findings in new ways.

or be altered by the process of observation. A three-dimensional digital projection of the brain allows students and researchers to explore neurological structures that would be destroyed in the process of observing them if a real-world brain were used.[19] In the humanities, digital technology is being used to "reconstruct" ancient art, artifacts, and monuments.[20] These new types of digital scholarship create both new challenges and pressures both for copyright law, since they are collaborative in a wholly new way, and for traditional scholarly publishing.

As new forms of digital scholarship grow and gain acceptance, another impact of the digital revolution on scholarship becomes apparent—the declining importance of traditional intermediaries like journal and book publishers. For centuries, scholars and publishers have lived in a symbiotic relationship that, if not entirely comfortable, was at least workable and provided mutual rewards. "Publish or perish" was the rule for scholars in academia, and publishers provided the outlets for those required tenure articles and books. Over time, the relationship between the publishing industry and academics has grown more contested, especially as more academic journals moved to commercial publishing houses and rapid price increases put unbearable strain on library budgets.[21] But digital scholarship, with the promise of new ways to conduct and present research, really shows the fissures in the conventional system. Traditional publications, even in their current online iterations, simply cannot handle a digital map of the brain or a virtual reconstruction of a Roman villa. They can publish articles about those projects, of course, but even their online databases are not equipped to actually disseminate the new scholarly creations themselves.

19. See "Thanatos4" 2006 for a forum on digital brain mapping that discusses some of the developments in this area.

20. See, for example, Forte 2000. Video examples of digital archaeology can be found in Ferreri 2013.

21. For statistics on the impact of increasing journal prices, as well as a discussion of digital access options, see Bosch and Henderson 2013.

And of course, traditional publications are not needed for that purpose. The Internet works fine as a distribution mechanism for these new works, which are born digital and based on visual technologies rather than print, without intermediation. Indeed, open distribution even of traditional works of scholarship, especially journal articles, is becoming a common option. Such "open access" may be accomplished through individual or institutional websites, public access databases like PubMed Central from the National Library of Medicine,[22] or a traditional publisher's open-access option. The difference is that traditional publication and open access on the Internet are both options for text-based scholarly articles, while the Internet, with or without access controls, offers the sole alternative for digital reconstructions, visualizations, and the like.

The digital revolution and Internet distribution options offer an alternative to the business model of traditional publishing, especially in the area of scholarly journal articles. Printed publication has traditionally been premised on an "economics of scarcity," and with good reason. When costs of reproduction and distribution were high, the need for intermediaries to underwrite those costs and then recoup their investment through sales was obvious. In order to prevent competition that might drive sale prices below the cost of production, copyright was necessary to provide a limited monopoly. By its nature, intellectual property is not diminished as it is distributed; I can locate and read a poem by Seamus Heaney without depriving others of that pleasure. But for Heaney to be able to make a living as a traditionally published poet, control of the reproduction and distribution of his work needs to be regulated; otherwise, prices would be driven down toward zero. If that happened, it would cease to make sense for publishers to continue printing and selling his books.

---

22. In 2008, the National Institutes of Health began requiring that publications based on research funded by the NIH be made openly accessible to the public in the PubMed Central database. For an overview of this policy, the largest open-access mandate in the United States to date, see NIH 2014.

This is the traditional justification of copyright regulation,[23] and it makes good sense when we are talking about an economy where printing and distribution costs entail scarcity. But in a digital world, this is not the case; reproduction and distribution have become easy, instantaneous, and cheap; the Internet offers an economy of abundance, and copyright does not always make sense in that world. Heaney may still need a traditional publisher to make a living, and he will therefore want to keep his poems off the open Web, at least for the most part.[24] But many other creators, including most academics, do not make money from their publications, and for them the move from an economy of scarcity to one of abundance offers an opportunity rather than a threat.[25] Copyright, in this new digital economy, is much more of a two-edged sword; it can still help authors and other creators maintain some control over their works, but it is often a hindrance to those who want to exploit digital opportunities to the fullest.

Because of the new opportunities created by digital technologies, the problem of access to scholarly works has become much more acute and noticeable. The price increases referred to above have meant for many years that libraries have had to cancel journal subscriptions on a regular basis. This naturally diminished access to scholarship; it became harder and harder to locate articles in certain journals that were either very expensive or used rarely enough that their costs could no longer be justified. But the possibility of digital distribution has put this access problem in deep relief. Because scholars can often find the materials they need online, many look there first when they are researching a topic, and some

---

23. By far the best source for understanding the economic structure of the copyright incentive system is Landes and Posner 2003.

24. It should be acknowledged, however, that an increasing number of "commercial" creators, including musical groups like Radiohead and Nine Inch Nails, are using open Internet distribution as a way to create a greater market for sales and for live concerts. It is much too simple to suggest that the free Web and profit making are incompatible; it is rather just a matter of time until new business models evolve.

25. As has already been noted, this analysis applies primarily to journal articles. The area of scholarly book publishing is more variegated and subject to a somewhat different analysis, although the potential for digital distribution and access is significant there as well.

seldom look anywhere else. Research done in this way may miss material in subscription-only databases that are not "crawled" by Internet search engines, or conversely, it may uncover material in such databases to which the researcher does not actually have access. Also, researchers may be restricted by the terms of publication contracts from improving this situation by distributing their work on the Internet. So the access "crisis" that began with spiraling journal costs has been deepened by copyright and contract restrictions that sometimes prevent scholars from making their work available digitally in a way that is readily accessible to others. In today's scholarly world, if one's work is not readily available on the Internet, it is effectively invisible.

It seems impossible to end this quick review of the impact of digital technologies on scholarship without acknowledging an issue that is raised by much of the preceding discussion, the future of peer review. The system of scholarly communication as a whole is heavily dependent on peer-review processes that are administered by publishers. As traditional publishing becomes less important, and indeed proves incompatible with many new forms of digital scholarship, scholars, universities, and scholarly societies must struggle to imagine new forms for the certification of quality scholarship and the evaluation of scholars. These discussions are well underway, even if no definitive new models have yet emerged.

In 2006, the Modern Language Association published a report, *On Evaluating Scholarship for Tenure and Promotion,* that directly confronted some of the challenges posed by scholarly works in new media. The recommendations made in this report call for "a more capacious conception of scholarship" and the explicit recognition of "the legitimacy of scholarship produced in new media."[26] That same year, the journal *Nature* sponsored an extensive online forum on peer review. The twenty-plus articles that make up this debate explore the current situation in depth and suggest diverse alternatives to the current publisher-dependent sys-

---

26. MLA 2006, 5. For the full discussion of new media, see pages 44–47. A summary of the recommendations is found on pages 5–6.

tem.[27] Among the many alternatives to the current system are peer-review systems managed more locally, perhaps by scholarly societies, whose incentives to evaluate new media projects would not suffer from the lack of monetary return, as do those of publishers, and post-publication review systems. In this latter category are included "crowd-sourced" systems, where user comments, reuse in new projects, number of downloads, and number of links to a work are all potential measures of quality and impact on the scholarly community.

The rise of online "mega-journals" like *PLOS ONE* from the Public Library of Science is another piece in the puzzle of re-visioning peer review. For this well-established and increasingly influential journal, as well as new experiments like *eLife*, peer review focuses only on the issue of scientific validity. Reviewers are not asked to evaluate the importance of the research since *PLOS ONE* is not seeking the traditional type of journal impact, which is based only on citation in other journals. Many more articles reflecting valid science are published, therefore, and the publication process is much quicker. This does not mean, however, that impact is not measured; it is simply evaluated after the fact, using "alternative metrics" (alternative to the impact factor) that look at how the article is cited and used across a broader range of sources, including other online journals, websites, blogs, and social media.[28] The rise of these so-called "alt-metrics" and their ability to measure impact on policy and practice as well as later scholarship are inevitably beginning to broaden and revise the traditional process of assessing scholarship for promotion and tenure.

27. The debate, with links to the full text of all the papers, can be found at www.nature.com/nature/peerreview/debate/index.html.
28. For a discussion of these alternative metrics, see Priem et al. 2011.

LIVING IN REVOLUTIONARY TIMES

By now it should be clear that the convergence of two revolutionary changes—the shift to automatic copyright protection and the explosion of digital technologies and the Internet—has tremendously complicated the situation for scholarly practice. William Patry's (2009, 6) observation that "While copyright laws are intended to be the principal vehicle of control, the Internet has largely thrown that control out the window" is as true for academic and scholarly works as it is for the music and movies about which Patry is writing. By way of summarizing the problem, we can identify three strands of complexity and conflict that a modern scholar concerned about intellectual property rights (and all scholars should be so concerned) has to consider.

First, tensions between authors and intermediaries often develop over who should control decisions about how works are distributed in new digital ways. One example of this tension is the lawsuit that is going forward as this is being written against Georgia State University, brought by publishers seeking royalty payments for works made available to students via electronic reserves or through course management systems.[29] A different but equally pertinent example of this struggle is the dispute over who should decide about e-book publication of older works: the publisher of the original print work or the family of the author.[30]

Another potential area of concern and conflict is the need to identify early in the process of disseminating scholarship the opportunities that will be important through the life of the work. While it used to be a safe

29. The case, Cambridge University Press, Oxford University Press and Sage Publications v. Carl Patton, Ronald Henry, Carlene Hurt and J.L. Albert, was filed on April 15, 2008, in the Federal District Court for the Northern District of Georgia and decided in favor of Georgia State in May 2012. The trial court held that seventy of the seventy-five short excerpts from books that were made available to students in specific GSU classes were not infringing because they were "fair use." The publishers have appealed that decision, and that appeal is pending, as of this writing, in the 11th Circuit Court of Appeals.

30. One example of such a dispute is described in Rich 2009.

assumption that print publication was a sufficient and comprehensive way to distribute a work, it is now necessary to consider all kinds of digital opportunities. The fact that traditional publication usually involves a transfer of copyright and the retention by the author of some set of circumscribed rights means that a certain amount of prescience is necessary to avoid signing a publication contract that will severely limit reuse and new opportunities in the future.

Finally, there is simply a good deal of uncertainty about the copyright status of many new forms of scholarship. Scholars may not know who really owns all of the rights in a digital reconstruction of an ancient monument or a three-dimensional scan of a commercially purchased model of the human skeleton. Likewise, it may be unclear who is entitled to transfer rights for certain types of work and how others may be permitted to use works that are distributed on the Internet. As various types of licensing (a way to permit uses of intellectual property without transferring the rights) proliferate, a confusion of permissions and restrictions increasingly bewilders and frustrates academic authors and scholars.

In the pages that follow, we will attempt to untangle some of these threads and clarify the various issues around intellectual property rights in scholarship. We will begin by examining the notion of intellectual property itself, since even the name is somewhat contested, and explicating the different forms that intellectual property protection takes: copyright, trademark, and patent. After that we will look closely at the issue of who actually owns the IP rights in scholarly work; issues of work made for hire, joint creation, and the application of institutional IP policies will be discussed.

Once we have a clearer notion of what IP rights are and who owns them, we will turn to the issue of using other people's protected works to create new scholarship. Here we will examine both specific exceptions for teaching and the much more commodious fair use exception, which is the cornerstone both of everyday scholarly practices like quoting a previous author in a new book or article and of innovative types of "remix" scholarship.

The next two chapters focus on the dissemination of scholarly work. The first will discuss copyright management for scholarly authors and consider the benefits and risks of the burgeoning open-access movement. We will look at specific language from publication agreements and consider its impact on opportunities for scholars to increase their impact in their fields. Then we will turn, in chapter 6, to a couple of the ways in which newer means are being used to control online distribution that go beyond copyright protection per se. One such development is the proliferation of licenses in the online environment that directly address the questions of how others can and cannot use works that are distributed on the Internet. Here we will consider the regime of online licensing known as the Creative Commons, as well as licenses on commercial "Web 2.0" sites that may influence decisions about whether or not they offer suitable methods for distributing scholarship. We will also briefly discuss the use of technological measures, so-called digital rights management, that govern uses of online content without any direct reference to intellectual property law.

In the final chapter we will consider international issues, recognizing that the Internet is unavoidably and blessedly global, but also considering some of the less felicitous impositions, such as the legal protection for those digital rights management systems that have sprung up in US law due to international agreements. We will examine the provisions of the major international treaties and discuss how effective national law and international negotiations can be in the online world. Then, by way of conclusion, we will look at some of the unsettled issues in digital IP, the unfolding of which will likely continue to complicate and influence the way scholarship is carried out in the twenty-first century.

This book is written explicitly for scholars and is intended to facilitate day-to-day activities that scholars engage in, including the creation of scholarly works, teaching, and publication. Because copyright is the aspect of intellectual property law that is a common concern for scholars in all denominations (as opposed, for example, to patent law, which impacts a smaller segment of the academy), the heavy emphasis is on that aspect of intellectual property law. For scholars who must navigate patent or trademark issues, there are usually offices available on campus to assist them; such offices are usually called tech transfer, licensing and commercialization, or some similar appellation. But copyright law impacts every scholarly production, from classroom PowerPoint slides to journal articles to online class videos. For that reason, copyright is the main topic discussed in these pages. Although the goal is to provide practical information related to these ubiquitous activities, because the audience is scholars, it seems good to provide enough background to encourage deeper reflection than the average how-to book might provoke. Hence the deliberate effort to create a "handbook" that is both practical—the examples especially offer very concrete discussion of specific problems—and yet theoretical enough to satisfy the academic mindset.

What Is Intellectual Property Law and Why Does It Matter?

THE MAJORITY of this book will address copyright issues that are, or should be, of concern to academics and other scholars. But copyright law is only one of several types of intellectual property regulation. Scholars do encounter patent and trademarks issues in the course of their work, and we will discuss those other types of intellectual property rules as we proceed. In order to understand the contours and the limitations of copyright and to prepare for those later discussions, it is useful to examine and compare the three major types of IP protections side by side. Patent, trademark, and copyright laws all provide some exclusive entitlements to products of the intellect, but otherwise they differ a great deal in justification, scope of protection, and means by which that protection is obtained and enforced.

The kinds of questions that arise for those who advise scholars on intellectual property matters often indicate the types of confusion that must be addressed by a careful taxonomy of these legal regimes. When academics or their students wonder if they might infringe copyright by referring to Coca-Cola on a website for a marketing class, or if the phrase "Got Milk?" is "copyrighted" so that others cannot use variations on it (which seem to abound, especially among student groups), they are confusing copyright with trademark protection. Likewise, worries about using someone else's "copyrighted ideas" or preventing someone from using my protected ideas conflates copyright, often called "soft" protection because it does not encompass underlying ideas, with patent protection, which is "hard" and does protect the idea that underlies a patented invention.

Because superficial similarities, including the use of the umbrella term *intellectual property*, often mask profound differences such as these, it is important that we treat each of these IP regimes in a consistent and systematic way. After some initial reflections on the use, and frequent misunderstanding, of the term *intellectual property*, we will approach each of the three major types of protection by asking these five questions:

- Why is this form of protection offered?
- What exactly is being protected?
- How is protection obtained?
- How long does the entitlement last?
- How is the protection enforced?

After we have discussed these questions in regard to copyright, patents, and trademarks, we will take a very quick look at one final form of IP regulations, which is of much less importance to scholarship, the law of trade secrets.

IS "INTELLECTUAL PROPERTY" THE RIGHT NAME?

Intellectual property is usually seen as a general term that refers to products of invention or creativity that do not exist in tangible form. Even this broad definition, paraphrased from the *Oxford English Dictionary*, is difficult to square with the actual forms of intellectual property *protection*, since both copyright and patent protection require a tangible embodiment of the work. But the real objection to the phrase *intellectual property* is that it implies an analogy with more traditional forms of physical property, and that analogy is deeply flawed, at least as it is often used in polemics. The problems with the analogy can be approached from two different perspectives; on the one hand, intellectual property has characteristics significantly different from real property, and on the other, real property ownership is subject to far more exceptions and limitations than is often acknowledged.

In *Moral Panics and the Copyright Wars*, William Patry (2009; see especially chapter 3) observes that this misleading parallel to physical property is often used by proponents of stricter copyright protection to liken infringement to theft. Downloading a song is analogous, in this view of the matter, to stealing a car. But as soon as this analogy is drawn, its weakness is obvious. When my car is stolen, I am left without transportation, and the cost for me to obtain a new car will be quite high. On the other hand, if a song I wrote is downloaded without authorization, I am nevertheless not deprived of the song. Indeed, the greater availability that has been created may actually increase the value of that which I still retain, the original song. In economic terms, this type of good (like a song) is referred to as "non-rivalrous," which means that consumption does not deplete the supply of intellectual productions, and the "marginal cost" of creating more copies of those productions is near zero.[1]

A slightly different economic characteristic of intellectual property is that it is "non-excludable," meaning that the non-rivalrous proliferation of copies makes it impossible to exclude those who do not pay from gaining access to the works. Copyright and other IP restrictions are intended to solve this "free-rider" problem and to artificially impose excludability on works of creativity and inventiveness. The reason for this restriction on intellectual productions that makes them act more like traditional physical goods in the marketplace is to provide an incentive for artists, writers, and inventors to continue to create.[2] Copyright and patent laws

---

1. For an explanation of non-rivalrous and non-excludable goods, see Stiglitz 1999, 308–25.

2. This, at least, is the purpose behind copyright and patent regulation. As we will see, the reason for allowing trademark exclusivity is quite different.

create limited monopolies that are intended to strengthen the market power of those who hold these rights so that they can make money and will be encouraged to keeping creating and inventing.

Once we recognize the flaw in the analogy between intellectual property and other types of property and the role of IP regulation in making the one seem more like the other, we are left with a dilemma about how and when to employ the language of property.[3] As we have already seen, those who would like to see more and stronger legal regulation for IP tend to encourage the use of the physical property analogy, while those who think, like Patry, that we already protect IP so strictly that we are actually harming creativity and innovation criticize the ubiquitous comparison. It is worth noting that even the most classic forms of property ownership are not really as absolute as "maximalists" sometimes assert that IP protection should be.[4] The ownership of land, for example, is subject to a whole raft of legal restrictions and exceptions, including taxation, adverse possession rules, zoning regulations, and the state's power of eminent domain. As copyright scholar James Boyle (2008, 8) writes, there are two approaches to dealing with the property analogy for intellectual creations: "One can reject it and insist on a different and 'purified' nomenclature, or one can attempt to point out the misperceptions and confusions using the very language in which they are embedded."

---

3. Lawyers, however, tend to enjoy this sort of dilemma; law professor David Lange (1981, 144) asserts in "Recognizing the Public Domain" that the distinctions between real and intellectual property are what "makes the [latter] subject challenging and fun."

4. Author Mark Halperin is perhaps the best current example of a full-scale maximalist in regard to copyright, thanks to his opinion piece in the *New York Times*, "A Great Idea Lives Forever. Shouldn't Its Copyright?" (2007) and his subsequent book *Digital Barbarism: A Writer's Manifesto* (2009). His assertions seem to be based more on an emotional sense of ownership than on economic logic, and the desire for copyrights that last forever is directly counter to the Constitutional foundation of these laws in the United States. Nevertheless, similar claims continue to be asserted in the pages of the *New York Times*, most recently by Scott Turow (2013), president of the Authors' Guild, in "The Slow Death of the American Author."

Throughout this book, then, we will continue to refer to intellectual property when we mean the general category of intangible creations protected by copyright, patent, or trademark rules. Whenever that term is used, however, it should be understood to be subject to the twin qualifications that the analogy with real, tangible property is potentially misleading and that even tangible property rights are never absolute. With these qualifications in mind, the discussion of the specific justifications and structures of copyright, patent, and trademark regulations that follows will, perhaps, not seem as strange and counterintuitive as it otherwise might.

COPYRIGHT

Purpose and Character

Copyright law is a creature of the age of printing and was originally intended, in England at least, to maintain royal control over this new technology and protect the monopoly held by the Stationers' Company, which represented the publishers of the day. In the sixteenth century, stationers literally bought manuscripts from authors and then received from the Crown the exclusive right to print copies of those manuscripts, assuming the king approved of the content. No one else was allowed to print copies, thus ensuring that only authorized works acceptable to the state would circulate. Thus the earliest form of copyright was quite literally a right to make copies.[5]

The earliest English copyright statute, in 1709, ostensibly gave the right to authorize copies to the authors, rather than directly to the stationers, but it did not significantly change the system, since authors still had to sell that right to stationers in order to have their works printed. The

---

5. For the earliest history of copyright, see Patterson 1968, especially chapter 4, "The Stationer's Copyright."

exclusive right given to authors by this law, called the Statute of Anne (8 Anne, c. 19 (1709)), was restricted to a period of fourteen years with the potential for a living author to renew for an additional fourteen years; after that time (twenty-eight years maximum), anyone could print copies of a work. When a similar law was enacted in the new United States of America, authors of books, maps, and charts were also given "the sole right and liberty of printing, reprinting, publishing and vending" for a renewable term of fourteen years.[6]

The authority for Congress to pass that initial copyright law, and all subsequent copyright and patent laws, comes from a clause in the US Constitution. In enumerating the powers of Congress, Article 1, Section 8 of the Constitution includes authorization for Congress "to promote the progress of science and the useful arts, by securing for limited times to authors and inventors the exclusive right to their respective writings and discoveries." Unlike every other enumerated power of Congress, this one comes with an explanation of the rationale behind it, perhaps because not all of the Founding Fathers thought these limited monopolies were a good idea.[7] Whatever the reason, however, this clause states the justification for providing legal, monopolistic protection to intellectual property; it is done to promote learning and invention. Another way to say this is that these exclusive rights create a market—where otherwise the non-rivalrous and non-exclusive nature of intellectual creations might prevent an effective market—and the rewards from this market are intended to provide an incentive for authors to write and inventors to invent. Copyright and patent laws can thus be judged based on their effectiveness in achieving this goal of promoting innovation.

---

6. The first US Copyright Act is 1 Stat. 124, enacted in the second session of the First Congress.

7. For a discussion of the reservations held by Thomas Jefferson regarding intellectual property laws, see Boyle 2008, 17–27.

What Can Be Protected?

Copyright protection now extends much further than the "books, maps and charts" mentioned in 1790; the subject matter of copyright now includes these eight broad categories:

(1) literary works;

(2) musical works, including any accompanying words;

(3) dramatic works, including any accompanying music;

(4) pantomimes and choreographic works;

(5) pictorial, graphic and sculptural works;

(6) motion pictures and other audiovisual works;

(7) sound recordings; and

(8) architectural works.[8]

As extensive as this list is, it is subject to an important qualification. Copyright protects the expression of an idea but not the idea itself.[9] This is sometimes referred to as "soft" intellectual property protection. Because ideas are not protected, genuinely independent creation does not give rise to infringement of copyright. If I sit at my word processor and write a poem that is identical to one written by US Poet Laureate Charles Wright without ever having seen his work, I have not infringed his copyright (although a court might have a very hard time believing that I really had never had access to Wright's poetry).[10]

---

8. The US copyright law is found in Title 17 of the United States Code. Reference to specific provisions within that law are written as, for example, "17 U.S.C. § 102," where the second number refers to the specific section. Section 102 is where this list of subject matter is found.

9. This is stated explicitly in 17 U.S.C. § 102(b).

10. There was a well-known copyright infringement case involving George Harrison's song "My Sweet Lord" in which a court ruled that Harrison was liable for infringement even though the court acknowledged that the copying (of the Chiffons' hit song "He's So Fine") was unintentional. This decision, in Bright Tunes Music v.

Truly independent creation of similar works is quite rare, of course, but the refusal to protect ideas under copyright has a more important consequence for scholars, since it underlies the difference between copyright infringement and plagiarism. To put that difference in a nutshell, copyright infringement is the unauthorized use of the work of another (if that work is protected by copyright), while plagiarism is the unacknowledged use of another's work. A single reuse of someone else's work can be both plagiarism, because unacknowledged, and copyright infringement, if the work is protected and the use does not fit into any of the copyright exceptions. But a use also might be infringement without being plagiarism, since acknowledgement (citation) will cure the latter but does nothing to mitigate infringement. Similarly, use of a work that is no longer protected by copyright will never constitute infringement but may still be plagiarism if there is no acknowledgement of the source. Finally, to return to the point at which we started this discussion, copying ideas from someone else's work without acknowledgement is usually plagiarism, even though there is no copyright in the ideas that could be infringed. An example of this possibility is the 2006 lawsuit brought against the author Dan Brown in the United Kingdom for allegedly using ideas from an earlier nonfiction work as the foundation for his book *The Da Vinci Code*. Brown was acquitted of infringement charges because he had borrowed only ideas, not protectable expression, from the earlier work.[11]

In addition to excluding ideas from its subject matter, copyright law also does not protect short phrases and titles. Thus it is perfectly possible for two books to have the same title. To offer just one example of this, a

---

Harrisongs Music 420 F. Supp. 177 (SDNY 1976), stands as testimony to the difficulty of proving independent creation. But see also the famous dictum asserting the possibility of such creation by Judge Learned Hand in Sheldon v. Metro-Goldwyn Picture Corp., 81 F.2d 49, 51 (2nd Cir. 1936).

11. The case was decided on April 7, 2006, by Mr. Justice Peter Smith in the British High Court of Justice, Chancery Division. It should be noted that plagiarism, unlike copyright infringement, is not a legal offense, although it is often a firing offense for academics.

quick library catalog search reveals that a 2009 book by Barbara Bradley Hagerty called *Fingerprints of God* shares that title with a 2000 work by Robert Farrar Capon. Whatever marketing difficulties may be caused by these identical titles, there is no legal infringement. The only situation in which a title or short phrase might be protected under intellectual property laws would be if the phrase was or contained a trademark, about which we will say more at the end of this chapter.

Exclusive Rights

Apart from these exceptions, all original works of authorship that fall within these eight broad categories receive copyright protection. That protection consists of five exclusive rights that are held, initially, by the author or creator and that can be transferred or licensed by her. All authors have the exclusive right to authorize reproduction (copying), distribution, public display, public performance, and the making of derivative works from the original. A separate exclusive right is granted in the case of sound recordings, to authorize performance of the work publicly by means of digital audio transmission.[12] The contours of these rights will be discussed as we move through our topics, but some examples will help illustrate the general logic of copyright.

Obviously, a book author has the right to forbid or allow copies of his work to be made and sold, and he can (and probably must) transfer that right to a publisher. That author also has the sole right, until and unless it is given to the publisher, to authorize the making of a translation of his book, or a film treatment. This derivative works right is very important for scholars, whose later work almost always builds, in some way, on work they have done previously. In addition to these rights, artists and others who create works meant for display have the authority to allow or forbid such display; this right is qualified by an authorization for the owner of a particular work to display that work at the physical location

---

12. These exclusive rights are enumerated in 17 U.S.C. § 106.

(e.g., a museum) where it is kept. Rights holders in plays, movies, and even poems (among other kinds of works that are typically performed) have the same power to permit or prevent performances. Rights holders can control only public performances, not those that take place privately. Thus I can screen a movie in my home for viewing by my friends and family but may not show the same film in a public place or to an audience beyond my social acquaintances without authorization.[13]

A film showing that takes place in classroom provides a particularly relevant example for scholars of how these rights and exceptions work together. To begin with, a filmmaker or production company holds the right to authorize or prevent public performance of its films. A classroom performance for students clearly falls within the definition of a public performance given in the Copyright Act (see 17 U.S.C. § 101), so without authorization, such performances would be infringing. But it would be inefficient to the point of impossibility for professors to seek permission each time they want to show a film, and a rule that required that would be harmful to education. So the Copyright Act incorporates a specific exception that allows classroom performances as part of "face-to-face teaching activities" (17 U.S.C. § 110(1)). As long as the film used is a lawfully made copy (i.e., not bootlegged), the performance can proceed without permission from the copyright holder. Since this is an exception to the public performance right, however, it does not extend to making copies of the film. If, for example, the professor wants to compile clips of different films onto a new DVD to use in a classroom, that activity must either be justified by a different exception in the copyright law—fair use is a likely candidate (17 U.S.C. § 107)—or it can be done only with permission from the rights holder.

---

13. Authorization to exercise one of the rights in copyright may come in the form of permission from the rights holder, but it may also come from an explicit exception written into the law, as the following paragraph illustrates.

How Protection Arises

These exclusive rights are held by the author or other creator from the very moment of creation; they arise automatically as original work is fixed in tangible form. We have already discussed this automatic protection at some length, but two additional points should be made here.

First, the standard of originality for copyright is very low. A case from the United States Supreme Court in 1991 established that the white pages of a phone book, which contain only factual material arranged in a very obvious way—alphabetically—was not sufficiently original to be subject to copyright protection (Feist Publications, Inc. v. Rural Telephone Service Co., 499 U.S. 340 (1991)). From the fact that the Supreme Court had to intervene and reverse the lower court in this case, we can see that this was a close call and that most works showing even a little more originality than a phone book (the Supreme Court uses the phrase "a modicum of creativity") will be subject to copyright. This means that virtually all of the production of a scholar, from lecture notes and written field observations to book and article manuscripts, are potentially eligible for copyright protection. It also means that the default assumption must be that most of the material we find on the Internet is subject to someone else's copyright and cannot be freely used without authorization, either from the rights holder or based on an exception within the copyright law.

The other point to make about automatic protection is that formalities are no longer required. As we have already said, the days when notice of copyright in the form of the symbol © had to be placed on works in order to establish protection ended in 1992. Also, registration of a copyright is no longer needed to gain protection, although it is still a requirement before one can enforce the rights against an alleged infringer. An example may help clarify this divided regime, where protection is immediate but enforcement depends on registration. As soon as the words I am writing appear on the screen and are saved in my computer's memory, they are protected by copyright as original expression fixed in tangible form. If that copyright is infringed, however, I (or my publisher) would have to register the copyright before going to court. The protection exists prior to registration, or else it could not have been infringed, but registration—a formal acknowledgement by the government of that pre-existing protection—is required before a federal court will hear the lawsuit over infringement (17 U.S.C. §§ 401–412).

Copyright Term and the Public Domain

The Constitutional clause cited above states that these exclusive rights that Congress is allowed to bestow must be "for limited times." The term of protection for copyright has grown longer with virtually every revision of the copyright law, from fourteen years in 1709 to the current term of life of the author plus seventy years. As I write these words, I am fifty years old; since actuarial projections suggest I can expect to live another twenty-five years, the protection for this work will likely last ninety-five years, well into the twenty-second century.

When the US term of copyright was extended from life plus fifty to life plus seventy, the Supreme Court was asked to declare that action incompatible with the Constitutional requirement that copyright be used to promote innovation. In a case called *Eldred v. Ashcroft* (537 U.S. 186 (2003)), the court held that nearly any term short of forever—that is, that is "limited" in some way, even when applied retroactively—is within the Constitutional authority of Congress. There is ample evidence, however, that extensions of the term of copyright have long ceased to serve any incentive function for authors and creators. It is hard to image that F. Scott Fitzgerald, for example, would have been more inclined to write his books if he had known that after his death the length of his copyright would be increased. Indeed, a recent study by Cambridge University economist Rufus Pollock (2009) concluded that the original term of fourteen years was actually pretty close to the optimal term of copyright protection. Nevertheless, the minimum term of protection is now set by international agreement at life of the author plus fifty years, and the United States has added twenty years to that (as, indeed, have many other nations).

Because copyright lasts for only a limited term, however lengthy, the period of protection does eventually expire and works enter the "public domain."[14] Once a work is in the public domain, none of the exclusive rights apply and all comers are allowed to do whatever they want with the intellectual property. Thus reprint editions of books can be published at cheaper prices, films can be colorized and shown over and over on television, and new works can be created out of older ones, in the style of Marcel Duchamp's famous mustachioed *Mona Lisa*.

Because of the many extensions of copyright's term, and the transition in the United States from a fixed period of years to a "life plus" system, it is often very hard to tell whether or not a work is still protected or is in the public domain. The only definitive rule for the United States is that a work published before 1923 is in the public domain. Works published between 1923 and 1977 may or may not still be protected, while works created thereafter are certainly within copyright.[15]

The public domain, of course, is not limited to works whose copyright has expired. As we have already seen, facts, titles and short phrases, and most importantly, the ideas embodied in copyrighted material are all in the public domain and available for reuse. Also, in the United States, works by the federal government are in the public domain because of an explicit provision of the copyright law that renounces protection for "any work of the United States Government" (17 U.S.C. § 105). This is a great boon to scholarship, but its scope must be carefully understood. First, it applies only to works by the federal government, not to those created by states. Second, it applies only to works created by regular federal employees in the course of their employment. Works by contractors or by grantees of the government will still be entitled to copyright protection, and that copyright can even be transferred to the government.

---

14. The public domain is simply defined as all material subject to intellectual property rights that is no longer so protected; see Boyle 2008, 38, and Lange 1981.

15. This quick summary is woefully inadequate; for help determining if a work is or is not still protected, the best resource is the Internet chart created, and updated annually, by Cornell University librarian Peter Hirtle (2014).

This point about grantees is especially important for scholars, whose research is frequently underwritten by grants from federal agencies such as the National Institutes of Health or the National Endowment for the Humanities. These grants do not give the government a legal claim in the copyright of work produced under them, although sometimes the terms of the grant will give the government a license to make certain uses of the work. But copyright remains with the grantee/author unless there is explicit agreement otherwise.

Infringement and Exceptions

A copyright is infringed when one (or more) of the exclusive rights is exercised, without authorization, by someone other than the rights holder. Authorization can be in the form of permission from the rights holder, which we call a license, or it can be found in the copyright statute itself, in the form of one of the many exceptions to the exclusive rights that have been specified by Congress. Most infringement disputes involve either a disagreement over whether or not a defendant had permission (a license) to do what he did or a controversy over the proper scope and application of one of the exceptions.

To prove infringement, a rights holder must show, first, that she holds a valid copyright. This is where registration of the rights is important and why it is required prior to bringing a lawsuit. Second, a rights holder must show that an infringing action took place. Sometimes this is a straight-forward question of fact; either an unauthorized public showing of a film took place or it did not. Most often, however, the issue is about alleged copying, and the rights holder must prove that the work in which she holds the rights was copied. Often, the fact of copying is itself disputed— remember our brief discussion of independent creation—so the courts look to see if the alleged infringer had access to the original work and whether there is "substantial similarity" between the copyrighted work and the new, allegedly infringing, creation.

Copyright infringement is a "civil action," which means that the private party who owns the rights has the privilege and obligation of bringing the lawsuit. The state does not prosecute copyright infringement in most cases. There is provision in the law for criminal prosecution, but it applies to cases of willful, widespread, and profitable counterfeiting of a type that should never involve legitimate scholarship.

Because infringement is a civil cause of action, the remedy for a rights holder whose copyright has been infringed is money damages. Again, there are criminal penalties available, but not in situations that this book addresses. Generally an aggrieved rights holder can get two major remedies—an injunction to stop the infringement and damages. Damages may either be based on the actual losses suffered by the plaintiff, either directly or measured by profits made on the infringement, or the plaintiff may elect damages that are set within the law. These "statutory" damages are available for a plaintiff only if the copyrighted work was registered with the Copyright Office within three months of its publication or at some time before the infringement began. Since proving actual damages is difficult and expensive, most infringement plaintiffs opt, if they can, for the statutory damages, which may range from as little as $750 per work infringed to as much as $150,000.[16]

One bit of good news for academics is that the damages provision of the Copyright Act contains a special provision saying that an employee of a nonprofit educational institution who commits an infringement based on a good faith (but mistaken) reliance on fair use, the most capacious and important of the copyright exceptions, shall not be liable for statutory damages (see 17 U.S.C. § 504(c)(2)). In those cases, only an injunction or actual damages will be available to the rights holder.

This mention of fair use brings us to the final topic in our whirlwind tour of copyright law, the exceptions to the exclusive rights. Fifteen sections of the Copyright Act (beginning with section 107, on fair use) and

---

16. This range of damages and the standards courts are to use in setting a remedy within it are set forth in 17 U.S.C. § 504.

almost 40 percent of its pages, are dedicated to exceptions. These usually have the form of statements that, in a particular situation, a described act is not an infringement, "notwithstanding" the provision that describes the exclusive rights. Several of these exceptions are directly aimed at the activities of scholars and teachers, and we shall discuss these in detail as we proceed. But here it is worth pointing out that, although these exceptions are described in a way that suggests they are boundaries to the exclusive rights, just the way a fence marks the boundary of a piece of real property, in practice they work as defenses. That is, one would raise an exception after being sued for infringement, arguing that in spite having taken the action that is disputed, it is not really infringing because of the exception.

This procedure is discouraging to many potential users of copyrighted material, since it involves the expense of a lawsuit and the risk of liability, although we should recognize that most positive rights have to be raised in this way. We sometimes speak of the "chilling effect" that the threat of litigation can have even on perfectly lawful, because authorized by exceptions in the law, uses of copyrighted material.[17] But we should also realize that the copyright exceptions can also discourage rights holders from bringing lawsuits out of the same fear of fruitless expense. In any case, litigation around fair use creates a road map that fosters pretty secure decision making about fair use in many cases, and recent court cases about fair use in the digital context have help define that road map a good deal.

Reliance on the copyright exceptions is always something of a risk analysis, based on how clearly a particular activity fits within the scope of an exception. This analysis is an inevitable part of the process of scholarship, even though it is sometimes not acknowledged or recognized. One of the major tasks of this book is to clarify the scope of these copyright exceptions in regard to major scholarly activities. At one extreme, perhaps

17. The Chilling Effects Clearinghouse at www.chillingeffects.org is an online clearinghouse for stories about how threats of litigation over alleged copyright infringement, even when unfounded, can inhibit perfectly legal activities.

the most common academic exercise of fair use, the use of short quotations from other writers in a book or article, is almost wholly uncontroversial; it is so clearly an application of the fair use exception that a rights holder would be foolhardy to bring a lawsuit over the practice.

Readers are to be congratulated for getting through this rather long and detailed review of copyright law. They should be assured that it could be much, much longer; a great deal of detail is excluded here because it is not directly relevant to our topic. But they can also take comfort in the fact that the review of patent and trademark laws will be much shorter. This is true, first, because much of those two bodies of law can be described by comparison with copyright. Also, copyright is by far the most important form of intellectual property protection from the point of view of scholarship. The comparative treatment of patents and trademarks that follows should make the reasons for that priority abundantly clear.

PATENTS

Researchers in many fields, from the hard sciences to computer programming and even in business schools, may produce inventions that are potentially subject to patents. Many patentable inventions arise from government-funded research, and since 1980, when the Bayh–Dole Act, which permitted colleges and universities to own and commercialize these patents, was adopted, patents have become increasingly important and profitable on campuses. This "hard" type of IP protection is quite different from copyright; it requires much more effort and expense to obtain, protects the idea behind an invention as well as its particular expression, and lasts for a maximum of only twenty years.

Purpose and Character

The same Constitutional clause that permits Congress to enact copyright laws is also the source for federal patent laws that protect inventors. Thus the justification for patent protection is also the same—patents are intended to "promote the progress of science and the useful arts" (U.S. Const. art I, § 8, cl. 8) by giving inventors an incentive to innovate and to share their devices and ideas with the public.[18] Beyond this similarity in purpose, however, the protection offered by patents differs dramatically from that of copyright.

The question of what can be protected by a patent is complex and controversial, but an important initial point is that, unlike copyrights, a patent protects the idea that underlies an invention. This is not to say that patent protection can be obtained for an abstract idea—it cannot—but only that "a well-drafted patent claim will protect the conception of an invention" (Medlen 1996, 25). Thus, once a patent has been granted, even an independent inventor who invents a process or machine that "reads on" the claims of the granted patent will be an infringer unless she has a license from the patent holder.[19] This is often referred to as "hard" IP protection, in contrast to the "soft" protection of copyright, which covers only expression and not underlying ideas. As law professors Rochelle Dreyfuss and Roberta Kwall (1996, 552) point out, this degree of protection really makes patents "the most desirable form of federal intellectual property protection" (for the rights holder, at least) because it gives the patent holder the "right to prevent *all* others from making the patented

---

18. US patent law underwent a significant revision with the passage of the America Invents Act of 2011. Among its central provisions that went in to effect in March 2013 was a new approach to defining the inventor entitled to a patent. Previously, the United States was almost alone in granting a patent to the first person to invent. This system required considerable investigation and argument over evidence of priority. Under the new law, the patent is award to the "first inventor to file," thus substituting the date of the patent application filing for the more contested date of invention.

19. A process or device "reads on" a patent claim when every element of the claim is present in the infringing process or device.

product or process or using it, selling it, or offering it for sale" (emphasis in original).

The US patent law, found in Title 35 of the United States Code, says that patents can be granted for "any new and useful process, machine, manufacture, or composition of matter, or any new and useful improvement thereof" (35 U.S.C. § 101). There are, broadly speaking, two major categories of patents—utility patents, which protect inventions and are the most common type of patent, and design patents, which protect original and non-obvious appearances given to products. We will focus here on utility patents because they are much more likely to be relevant to scholarly work.

For a patent to be issued four characteristics of the claimed invention must be found: it must be novel, non-obvious, useful, and "reduced to practice." Novelty for patents is different from the originality requirement for copyright, since *original* simply means not copied, whereas novelty requires that the basic concept behind the invention not have been expressed before. *Non-obvious* refers to the fact that a patent will not be granted if the idea for the invention would have been clear to anyone who looked at the "prior art" with the ordinary skills found in the invention's field of practice. Sometimes this is referred to as the requirement of an "inventive step."[20] The last two requirements, that the invention be useful and be reduced to actual practice, are what prevent abstract ideas from being patented. Indeed, part of the requirement for a patent application is that it disclose how the invention is made and used (called "enablement") and the "best mode (or embodiment)" for carrying out the invention. As we will see, this required disclosure is an important part of the balance between private protection and public use in the patent realm.

---

20. This usage is more common in other countries than it is in the United States, but it provides a helpful gloss on non-obviousness. For an example of a discussion of the inventive step, see the UK case of Biogen, Inc. v. Medeva PLC, decided in the House of Lords on October 31, 1996, [1997] RPC 1.

Scope of Patent Protection

The scope of a patent application is determined by the "claims" that are included in it; these claims are carefully crafted to assert the broadest scope possible (which makes the patent more profitable) without claiming so much that the application will be rejected. As Virginia Medlen (1996, 27) notes, these claims "constitute the core" of what a patent is able to protect and also determine how the courts will interpret the patent and decide infringement actions. The drafting of the claims is a highly specialized skill, involving a type of writing only a lawyer could appreciate. Here, for example, is the first of the enumerated claims from a patent application for "a sealed, crustless sandwich" which was first granted by the patent examiner but subsequently rejected by the Board of Patent Appeals:

We claim:
A sealed crustless sandwich, comprising:

a first bread layer having a perimeter surface coplanar to a contact surface;

at least one filling of an edible food juxtaposed to said contact surface;

a second bread layer juxtaposed to said at least one filling opposite of said first bread layer, wherein said second bread layer includes a second perimeter surface similar to said first perimeter surface;

a crimped edge directly between said first perimeter surface and said second perimeter surface for sealing said at least one filling between said first bread layer and said second bread layer;

> wherein a crust portion of said first bread
> layer and said second bread layer has been
> removed.[21]

This language may seem awkward and ridiculous, but patent attorneys have developed it over time to describe very exactly the scope of a particular invention and to guide courts in deciding when a patent has been infringed. The need to use this specialized language has the obvious effect of increasing the cost of obtaining a patent, since the services of an attorney or other patent specialist are nearly always required.

Scholars and Patented Inventions

There are two somewhat controversial applications of patent law that are important for scholars to be aware of, regarding software and business methods.[22] Software, interestingly, is potentially protectable both by copyright and patent. Because it is so much easier to obtain, most software developers rely on copyright to prevent copying of their work. But it is possible to get a patent for software in many cases, and it may be desirable to prevent competition where the underlying idea could be rendered through a variety of different "expressions" of code. "The key to successfully patenting software," writes Virginia Medlen (1996, 37), "is to describe in the application the integration of the software with generic hardware." Whereas a mere algorithm will not be eligible for patent protection, software code based on algorithms can be patented when it works with hardware to produce a "useful, concrete and tangible result" (see In Re Allapat, 33 F.3d 1526, 1544 (Fed. Cir. 1994) (en banc)).

---

21. Patent 6,004,596 (December 21, 1999). For a discussion of the history of this patent see Boyle 2008, xi, footnote 1.

22. A third controversial issue, over the patentability of genes, is pending before the Supreme Court at the time of this writing, in a case called Molecular Pathology v. Myriad Genetics, but that issue has less consequence for the broad range of scholars.

Protection for business methods has a convoluted history in US law. For most of its history, the Patent Office refused to issue patents for methods of doing business, seeing them as too abstract to meet the requirements for protection. This objection, of course, is very similar to that which would prevent software patents, and a 1998 case in the Federal Circuit, which is the appeals court for all patent issues in the United States, did a great deal to wipe away both the bar on software patent and that which prevented protection of business methods. In *State Street Bank & Trust v. Signature Financial Group* (149 F.3d 1368 (Fed. Cir. 1998)), the Federal Circuit reversed a lower court decision and found that a patent on a computer-based data processing system intended to structure investment decisions was valid. Since that decision, business method patents have become very common—Amazon.com holds a patent in the "1-click" online shopping method, for example (Hartman et al. 1999)—and there has been something of a backlash. In 2008 the Federal Circuit again cast doubt on the patentability of business methods in a case that rejected protection on a technique for hedging risks in trading of commodities (In Re Bilski, 545 F.3d 943 (Fed. Cir. 2008)). This continuing uncertainty is not really surprising since, as Professor Boyle (2008, 169) notes, "There is no evidence to suggest that we need a state-backed monopoly to encourage the development of new business methods."

Obtaining a Patent

Obtaining a patent is a complicated and expensive procedure. While copyright protection is automatic and registration of a copyright costs less than $100, patents require a lengthy application, go through a rigorous examination process, and cost thousands of dollars to get and maintain.[23] This difference is explained by the differences in the kind of protection

---

23. The current application and examination fee for a utility patent is $1,000. Maintenance fees, however, are required to keep a patent in force for its full term, and these fees total over $12,000.

each offers—soft versus hard—and the much greater potential for profit that a patent carries with it.[24]

The process of submitting a patent application nearly always requires employing an attorney, as the discussion of claims above should make clear. Not only does a patent attorney help write the various required parts of an application, he or she will also guide the application through the approval procedure. Each patent is rigorously considered by an examiner, who may seek more information, strike various claims or parts of claims, or reject the application altogether. Rejection of a patent application is often followed by an appeal to the Board of Patent Appeals. There are also sometimes "interference procedures" that attempt to reconcile claims in two different patents that appear to cover the same ground. Even after a patent has been granted, its validity can be challenged; indeed, the most common defense raised when someone is charged with patent infringement is the claim that the original patent should not have been granted.

Part of the application procedure requires that an inventor inform the patent examiner about "prior art," which means references to publications, products, or other publicly available information that anticipate the invention. This is in order to help the patent examiner assess the novelty and non-obviousness of the claims. In the United States, however, only relative novelty is required; anticipatory references in nonpublic sources, those from another country or that were published by the inventor herself less than a year before the application was filed, do not defeat a patent application. This can be an important point for scholars, who may well publish an article or dissertation prior to filing a patent application. Even submission of a single copy of a dissertation can start this clock running on novelty, so it is important to be aware of the rules of "relative novelty" and be certain that an application is filed within the one-year window after such publication.

---

24. It should be noted, however, that the great majority of patents that are granted never prove profitable.

These various disclosures, including the requirement that the patent application itself—which becomes a public document—explain exactly how to make the claimed invention, serve the basic public policy behind patents by making information about innovations readily available. The information thus available invites those who would like to license the patent invention as part of some new device or process, as well as those who seek to improve on what has been done before. Also, once the patent term expires, the invention or process is truly in the public domain because all of the background and creativity that went in to it have been revealed. As with copyright, the public domain marked out by patent law—by limits on patentable subject matter and by the expiration of the term of protection—is as integral to the purpose of the law as is protection itself.

Duration and Enforcement of Patents

The term of patent protection is much shorter than it is for copyright, perhaps because the protection granted is so much more complete. A utility patent lasts for twenty years, and a design patent for fourteen (see 35 U.S.C. § 154). To maintain protection for even this long, however, proactive steps must be taken and steep fees paid at three intervals during the life of the patent.[25]

It is only in its enforcement that patent protection is substantially similar to copyright. As in copyright, the patent holder has the exclusive right to license others to use, incorporate, and/or sell the patented product or process, and the patent is infringed when someone does one of these things without authorization. Again, this is a "private cause of action"; it is the rights holder, not the government, who brings a lawsuit charging someone with patent infringement. The remedies are also similar; the aggrieved rights holder can receive money damages and also get an injunction to stop the infringement. Since infringement of patents often

---

25. The fees that must be paid at 3.5, 7.5, and 11.5 years into the patent term are specified in the fee schedule (US Patent and Trademark Office 2014).

involves selling new products that incorporate some previously patented technology, an injunction could be financially devastating to a business; for this reason, injunctions really function as bargaining chips to force the second user to negotiate a licensing fee to be paid to the patent owner.

TRADEMARK

Purpose and Character

Trademark law protects the exclusive right to use specific words, phrases, names, and symbols in commerce to identify the source of goods or services. Because of this requirement that a trademark be used in commerce, it is the type of IP protection that impinges least often on scholarship, but it does sometimes have an impact. The justification for trademark protection is entirely different from the rationale behind copyrights or patents. Whereas the authority behind those bodies of law is found in the Constitutional clause, quoted above, that specifically authorizes IP regulation, trademark law is enacted under the powers granted in the so-called Commerce Clause.[26]

   This distinction in the Constitutional justification for trademark law is indicative of a very different purpose as well. While patents and copyrights exist to promote learning and culture, trademarks are essentially intended as consumer protection devices. Their primary purpose is to prevent consumer confusion over the source, and hence the quality, of goods and services they seek. By pointing exclusively to a consistent source, they reduce the time and effort that consumers must expend

26. The Commerce Clause is found in Article I, section 8, clause 3 of the US Constitution. The nation's first trademark laws were actually invalidated by the Supreme Court in 1878 because they could not be justified under the "Copyright clause" (art. I, § 8, cl. 8). See The Trademark Cases, 100 U.S. 82. Congress passed new laws around the turn of the twentieth century using its Commerce Clause power to regulate interstate commerce.

looking for what they want and, in theory at least, assure them of finding similar goods each time they buy a specific brand. When I want a cola drink, for instance, I am pretty confident that I know what I am going to get if I pop open a Coke. A secondary reason for granting protections for trademarks is to help businesses maintain the significant asset that is their name and reputation, referred to by economists as a company's "goodwill."

In the United States, the trademark law is also referred to as the Lanham Act, a piece of legislation that was adopted in 1946 and subsequently amended frequently. The Lanham Act is incorporated in Title 15 of the U.S. Code. Federal trademark law, however, is not exclusive, and many states also protect trademarks. This is a significant difference between trademark protection and that of copyrights and patents and results from the uncertainty about whether or not federal law can protect a "mark" that is used exclusively within a single state, since the Constitutional justification of the law is a power to regulate commerce "among the several states" (U.S. Const. art I, § 8, cl. 3).

Scope of a Trademark

As has been said already, trademark protection can cover both words and symbols. The McDonald's Corporation, for example, can prevent others from using both its name and the iconic golden arches. There has even been a court case involving insulation maker Owens-Corning in which the color pink was held to be a protectable trademark in the area of home insulation (In Re Owens-Corning Fiberglass Corp. 774 F.2d 1116 (Fed. Cir. 1985)).

Trademark protection is usually restricted, as this case indicates, to a particular area of commerce—a specific category of goods or services. The protection granted to Owens-Corning, for example, does not prevent another company from selling pink shoes because there is no competition between the two companies since they operate in wholly different markets.

In addition to its obvious and traditional role in preventing unfair competition, such as would result if a company other than Rolex started selling inferior watches and calling them by that protected brand name, trademark law also has a provision that prevents the "dilution" of famous marks. This gives added protection for a company's goodwill, even when the use that is objected to is not directly competitive. For example, the McDonald's Corporation successfully objected to a hotel that wanted to call one of its chains "McSleep Inns." The court found that consumers might be confused by this name, believing that the inns were owned or sponsored by McDonald's, even though the hotels would not directly compete with a McDonald's product (Quality Inns International, Inc. v. McDonald's Corp. 695 F. Supp. 198 (D. Md., 1988)). This protection is not uncontroversial because it can be seen as interfering with legitimate free speech interests and because it is so difficult to determine which trademarks should be considered famous. On this issue Stephen McJohn (2003, 282) writes:

> The federal dilution provision protects only "famous" marks, providing a list of factors to use in deciding whether a mark is famous. Some courts have been relatively undemanding with respect to famousness, such as holding that the famousness requirement is satisfied by being famous in a niche or regional market. But the trend seems to be toward demanding that the mark be well known among the public generally.

Trademark protection favors marks that are highly distinctive and easy to identify exclusively with a product or service. The more distinctive a word used as a trademark is, the more strongly it will be protected. Thus the best kinds of trademarks are coined words like *Kodak* or words that are arbitrary but have developed strong association with a particular product in the minds of consumers. In this category, consider "Scope" for mouthwash, where an ordinary word has a marketable association with a particular product, or "Hertz" for a car rental company, which was originally the owner's name but is now a very protectable trademark.

The more descriptive of a product or service a mark is, the harder it will be to get exclusive protection. "Budget" for a car rental company, for example, is less distinctive and more descriptive, ostensibly, than "Hertz" is, although the former was certainly chosen based on the benefit it would provide in marketing, even if it was somewhat less strong as a trademark. At the extreme of descriptiveness are generic words, which cannot be protected. I cannot obtain trademark protection for a beer called "Beer." In a similar way, the Remington company was denied a trademark on the phrase "Proudly Made in the U.S.A." because it was felt to be entirely descriptive and not sufficiently distinctive (In Re Remington Products, Inc., 3 U.S.P. Q. 2d 1614 (Trademark Trial and Appeal Board, 1987)).

The worst fate for a brand name is for it to become the generic description of the product so that it loses any claim to be distinctive and therefore protectable. This was what happened to the word *aspirin*, which was originally a brand name but has come to refer to any acetylsalicylic acid drug and which cannot be protected under trademark law. Companies often fight against a tendency toward becoming generic, which smacks of becoming a victim of one's own success. Thus Band-Aid maker Johnson & Johnson prefers to always say "Band-Aid brand adhesive bandages" in its advertising to make the point that *Band-Aid* is not a generic name for all bandages.[27]

Obtaining and Maintaining a Trademark

For a word or symbol to qualify for trademark protection, it must be used in commerce, although there is a provision in federal trademark law that allows for registration of a mark based on "intent to use" (15 U.S.C. § 1051(b)). As with copyright, federal registration is not a prerequisite to

---

27. For reinforcement of this point, see the Band-Aid website at www.band-aid.com (accessed May 9, 2013).

protection, but it provides substantial advantages for the mark holder. Trademark protection lasts for as long as the mark is used in commerce, although registration of the mark must be renewed every ten years. There is no time limit on how often a trademark registration may be renewed (15 U.S.C. § 1058).

With trademarks, the rule for ownership really is "use it or lose it" (see Foster and Shook 1993, 178). Maintaining a federal trademark requires filing an affidavit of continued use, and trademark protection is lost if the mark is abandoned,[28] or if it becomes generic. This is sensible in light of the purpose of trademark law to protect consumers; there is no longer any point to protection if consumers cease to identify the mark with one particular brand, and preserving protection would become, in that case, a pointless restriction on free speech.

Because a trademark can be lost if it is not used, is diluted too much, or becomes generic, it is important that trademark holders defend and protect their marks. This is another difference between trademarks and copyright. Copyright protection lasts for its full term unless it is explicitly renounced, and a copyright holder can sue the fourth infringer he encounters even if he did not sue the first three. A trademark, however, would be abandoned if the mark holder simply ignored infringements. This need to defend a mark sometimes leads to unfortunate litigation, where a mark holder will sue someone for infringement even where the second use is trivial or clearly noncompeting out of fear that the mark might be considered abandoned.[29]

As with the other forms of intellectual property, the enforcement of trademarks is a private cause of action, meaning that the mark owner must bring the lawsuit. Based on the purpose of trademark protection, the

---

28. There is a statutory presumption of abandonment of a trademark after two years of nonuse. See 15 U.S.C. § 1127.

29. Although what constitutes foolish litigation is a matter of opinion, to this author the lawsuit brought by the producers of the *Star Wars* movie against a protest group that used the same phrase to object to President Reagan's Strategic Defense Initiative seems to illustrate the danger. See Lucasfilm, Ltd v. High Frontier, 622 F.Supp. 931 (D.D.C. 1985).

standard for finding an infringement is whether or not consumer confusion will be caused by the second, challenged use of the same or a similar mark. If infringement is found, the owner of the trademark can get an injunction to prevent the second use and may also collect money damages.

Scholars and Trademark Use

Trademarks are probably the form of intellectual property protection that is of least relevance for scholars, but there are two situations in which they can impinge on scholarly work. The first involves university licensing, which is a significant source of revenue for many colleges and universities, especially those with well-known sports teams. Because universities license the use of their name and logo, trademark laws may restrict certain commercial uses that might lead to consumer confusion. My own employer, for example, might legitimately object if I used the university's name to advertise an independent consulting business that I ran because of the potential to imply university sponsorship and because it might dilute the lucrative market for licensed clothing and other products.

Even more relevant for most scholars, however, is the possibility that they will want to use trademarks from various businesses in their scholarly activities. Need one be concerned, for example, when writing a journal article that is critical of a particular corporation's practices in some area that the company will use trademark law to suppress the criticism? Or suppose that a scholar wants to create a website comparing corporate human resources policies and would like to use the logos of the companies to illustrate the site; is this permitted?

The answers to these questions rely on a couple of defenses to trademark infringement claims. These defenses are sometimes called fair use, but should not be confused with the statutory fair use exception in copyright law. The most relevant defense in trademarks, which would offer an answer to the questions above, is the defense for "nominative use," where the trademark is legitimately used to refer to the actual mark holder or its products. Most simply, I can advertise my car as a Mazda in a classified ad if it really is a Mazda (even though that is clearly a use in commerce); I can use the names of Coca-Cola and Hertz Rentals in this chapter because I am actually referring to those businesses. In an important case, a newspaper was held to be making a nominative, and therefore fair, use of the trademarked name of the "boy band" New Kids on the Block when it ran a poll asking readers to vote for their favorite New Kid (The New Kids on the Block v. News America Publishing, Inc., 971 F.2d 302 (9th Cir. 1992)).

One limit on this defense, however, is that the secondary user must not use more of the trademark than is necessary to accomplish the purpose of identification. Thus the article suggested above that criticizes a company will almost certainly be permitted—one of the reasons for this defense is to ensure that trademark cannot be used to suppress legal speech—but the use of logos on a website might be more doubtful and require some justification.

This free speech concern that underlies the fair use of trademarks extends even to parodies that would seem offensive and derogatory to the company. In a case that explicitly appealed to First Amendment values, the L.L. Bean Company was unable to enforce an injunction against an adult magazine publisher that published a short article entitled the "L.L. Beam [*sic*] Back-to-School-Sex-Catalog" (L.L. Bean, Inc. v. Drake Publishers, Inc. 811 F. 2d 26 (1st Cir. 1987)). This same free speech ideal is what prevents a trademark holder from using its exclusive rights in the mark to prevent critical websites that incorporate the company's name in the site's domain name. The classic example here is a website where the URL is some form of "www.companyXsucks" (see, e.g., http://walmartsucksorg.blogspot.com). The leeway given for nominative uses of a trademark, even when the use is critical or satiric, is important to protect academic freedom and support a robust discussion among scholars of issues involving commerce.

TRADE SECRETS AND THE ROLE OF IP IN SCHOLARSHIP

Trade secrets are fundamentally different from the other forms of intellectual property protection we have examined. The others—copyright, patent, and trademarks—all involve a form of creativity that depends for its value upon public disclosure. Such creativity either is protected or is a prerequisite for protection. Trade secrets, on the other hand, must be kept confidential. If a company discloses its secret, or even fails to take sufficient steps to safeguard it, trade secret protection is lost.

The most common forms of trade secrets are formulas for a product—Coca-Cola is the classic example here—and lists of a firm's customers.[30] These are types of corporate information that lose their value as soon as they are revealed, and there is little public interest in disclosure. For that reason, there is no federal legal regime that protects trade secrets. Instead, state unfair competition laws are the legal means for protecting such secrets. The usual remedies in lawsuits over a trade secret are temporary restraining orders and permanent injunctions to prevent the competitor from exploiting the misappropriated information.

In order to keep trade secrets confidential, companies often use nondisclosure agreements that employees or independent contractors must sign before gaining access to proprietary information. Scholars who do research through academic–corporate partnerships are most likely to encounter trade secret protection in the form of such nondisclosure agreements, or NDAs. It is also sometimes the case that an academic laboratory will want to keep certain research data confidential until analysis can be completed and publications prepared. Since raw data is not eligible for other kinds of IP protection, scholars occasionally resort to techniques similar to those used with trade secrets, including NDAs, to control release of data. Of course, such enforcement of confidentiality is temporary, because the ultimate purpose of academic research is publication in the broadest sense.

---

30. There is a nice discussion of trade secrets law in Medlen 1996, 39–45.

Indeed, with this discussion of trade secrets we have reached a kind of extreme in IP law that helps remind us of why IP matters, and how it sometimes hinders scholarship. In unfair competition situations, the need for protection and secrecy swallows up the concern for public access that animates copyright, patent, and trademarks.[31] For most scholarship, of course, the value of the work is inextricably bound up with access; the most scholarly book or paper ever written is worthless if no one reads it. For scholars, then, IP regulation functions primarily to structure the conditions for publication and to give the creators some control over that process. When IP regulations perform this function well, they are useful to scholars and scholarship; when, instead, they hinder access that would be advantageous to a scholar's work and reputation, they fail in their fundamental purpose.

It should now be clear why the principal emphasis for the remainder of this book will be copyright law. First, all scholars own copyrights in virtually all of the products of their work. Whereas patents require considerable effort and expense to obtain, copyright showers down on scholars as they write, record, and so on. And scholars seldom have access to competent advice about how to manage these rights. When a patent is involved, the inventor will almost always be working with a lawyer or with an academic office charged with "technology transfer," while copyright holders neither need nor can easily find similar expertise to help them make decisions. Second, copyright is inextricably bound up with publication and issues of how best to disseminate scholarship. In the complex environment for dissemination that now faces us because of digital opportunities, the choices that have to be made about how to manage copyright, when to license it, and when to agree to transfers are unavoidable. "Business as usual" in regard to these matters is no longer an option for scholars who seriously wish to make an impact on their

---

31. It is worth noting that the reason for wanting the public to have access may involve public policy, as it does with patents, or it may be because the work has no value unless the public can see and use it, as is the case with works protected by copyright and trademark.

chosen field of learning. Well-informed and thoughtful management of copyright has become a sine qua non for successful scholarship in the digital age.

Who Owns Scholarly Work?

THE QUESTION of who owns the various intellectual creations produced by scholars raises complex issues that are often frustrating and counterintuitive. One important principle is that ownership of copyright is always distinct from ownership of any physical instance of the copyrighted work; owning a book or photograph does not give me any copyright interest, and conversely, I may hold a copyright in a work even if I own no actual copies. Thus, for example, a painter or sculptor who sells her latest creation usually continues to own the copyright in it while the sole physical instantiation of the work becomes the property of her patron.

This principle underscores the unique nature of intellectual property and the complications it causes; while it is easy to decide who owns an automobile, which is tangible and cannot be reproduced without great effort, it may be much less clear who owns an intangible and non-rivalrous work like a poem, journal article, or idea for a new device.[1] Unfortunately, the vacuum of uncertainty created by this characteristic often results in oversimplified assertions about IP that are almost always incorrect. "Since I wrote it, it is mine" is one, some variation on which

---

1. For a discussion of the non-rival nature of intellectual property see chapter 2, section titled "Is *intellectual property* the right name?"

seems to be extremely common among scholars and accounts for the frequent tendency simply to ignore the provisions of copyright transfer agreements signed with publishers. On the other side of the coin, "Since I paid to have it created, it is mine" is an equally erroneous summary of the IP situation for scholarship.

Two unique aspects of academic creation must be considered as we struggle to untangle the puzzle of who owns scholarship. First is the ambivalent position that scholars find themselves in vis-à-vis intellectual creations, illustrated by the first oversimplified assertion above. The second is the clear tendency of intellectual property law to view all creative production as commodities, as suggested by the second oversimplification.

If we look back at the story of Finnian and Columba with which this book began, it is easy to see that the ambivalent attitude toward intellectual property in which the academics of our day find themselves is very old indeed. On the one hand, a particular work of the intellect is remarkably personal to its creator, and the desire to hoard and protect it is very strong. But academics and scholars are simultaneously creators and consumers of intellectual property; creation, in fact, depends on the ability to find, consume, and then reshape work that has gone before into new scholarship. While I may feel a strong desire to protect my own creation, I cannot afford to allow other creators that same luxury; I must have access to their work if I am to continue my own. And in any case, hoarding my work is counterproductive. The reason academics create is to share; reputations and career advancement depend on circulation. In this, scholarship shares a characteristic of all intellectual property; against all instincts to keep it secret, its value ultimately depends on making it known to others as widely as possible.

Even while creators think of their works almost like children, the law insists on treating those same works as commodities, subject to economic regulations (which is what our IP laws ultimately are), just as if they were integrated circuit chips or kumquats. The purpose of IP regulation is to create an economic incentive to create. It does this by establishing a limited monopoly, which allows prices to rise above the marginal cost of producing another copy. Thus, in theory, the creators can make enough money and will wish to continue to create more poems, scholarly articles, or widgets.

Intellectual property law generally does a poor job of accounting for any creative motivation outside the realm of economic motivation. Samuel Johnson famously said that "no man but a blockhead ever wrote, except for money" (Boswell 1925, 614). Even though his biographer immediately declared that this opinion sprang from Johnson's "indolent disposition" and could be refuted by numerous instances in the history of literature, this sentiment is really the foundation of US copyright law. Unfortunately (at least from the perspective of what the law supports), most academic writers find themselves in the company of Dr. Johnson's blockheads, since their motivations for creating scholarly works are seldom directly pecuniary. Work may be undertaken entirely for the sake of building a reputation or in hopes of securing a promotion or tenure and, thereby, some money. But our copyright and patent laws do not account very well for these nonfinancial or indirect motives. In her book on *Who Owns Academic Work?* Corynne McSherry (2001, 103) puts the issue succinctly when she writes, "Can faculty use a body of law designed to promote the distribution of intellectual commodities to resist the commodification of intellectual work?"

COPYRIGHTS AND PATENTS ON CAMPUS

Against this background of an ambivalent attitude toward intellectual property and the mixed motivations of many scholars, their employing institutions have discovered that patents and even copyrights offer a rich new vein of profit. The development of the university as a commercial space has really focused on patent ownership until quite recently. The passage in 1980 of the Bayh–Dole Act was an important step in that development (Pub L. No. 96-517 (1980), 35 U.S.C. §§ 200–211) since it made it possible for universities to own patents, and to retain the profits they generate, even when the inventions involved grow out of research funded by federal government grants. In subsequent years, patent ownership has become a major source of revenue for many institutions. University-owned patents generate almost $1 billion in profits (Blumenstyk 2003), and the largest university patent holder, the University of California system, ranked eighty-third, ahead of Nortel, Exxon Mobil, and the United States Navy, on the list of entities holding the most patents in 2009 (IPO 2009). Few universities can afford to ignore the potential profits of patent ownership, and "technology transfer" offices, with attendant policies that specify how costs and profits will be allocated, are now ubiquitous on campuses.

The value of copyrights has not been as obvious to most universities, and mechanisms to exploit that value have been slower to develop. It is relatively easy to keep track of the small number of patentable inventions being developed on a campus, but copyrightable material is created in great quantities every single day. Most of this copyrightable material has very little value apart from its immediate purpose. But the growth of the Internet, and especially the explosion of interest in distance education, has begun to suggest new categories of copyrightable works that seem to have value for universities apart from single uses and even independent of the scholarly identity of their creators. Material that is created for distance education classes, especially massive open online courses, or MOOCs, but also just as online supplements to traditional classes, offers new opportunities for universities to reevaluate the potential value of copyright ownership. Such materials allow schools to attract nontraditional students for whom schools do not bear the same support costs as for traditional students. Also, once a Web course is created, it can be repeated over and over, perhaps taught by a graduate student or adjunct professor. Thus copyright ownership for at least some types of faculty works seems to offer a source of reduced costs and maximized profits. Campus policies on copyright ownership, therefore, have become more nuanced and complex.

We will turn in a moment to specific issues associated with copyright ownership for scholars, and then to a discussion of what campus policies should look like. But before doing that, it seems worthwhile to make even more explicit the reasons that copyright and patents are treated so differently in academia.

As we have already discussed, the process for obtaining patent protection is much more complex and expensive than that for obtaining copyrights. Indeed, while copyrights are automatic, a patent often takes years to obtain, and it can cost tens of thousands of dollars to navigate the process. An individual need do nothing but fix his original expression in tangible form in order to obtain a copyright, while obtaining a patent is beyond the reach of most individuals acting on their own. Also, the process of developing a patentable invention usually involves heavy reliance on materials provided by a university. While computer software and processes may still be developed by a solitary inventor working in her garage, most other patentable inventions require extensive and expensive equipment, including laboratories and research assistants. Patents are therefore costly and rare; policies are consequently written to consider the institution's need to recoup investment and the inventor's need for support, both financial and legal, in pursuit of the protection.

Copyright, on the other hand, is everywhere on college campuses, and it requires no unusual effort at all to obtain protection. Every single person who can write or draw or snap a photograph owns a variety of copyrights under our current legal system, although most do not realize that they do. Thus campus copyright policies have to be much more sweeping, addressed to general categories of creation rather than specific circumstances, and covering all categories of employees, not just those who do research that could result in new inventions. The emphasis on copyright in this book is justified by this broad reach for copyright protection. That law, and the local policies adopted around it, apply to many more people than patent law does, and most campuses have few resources to help scholars, students, or staff manage the copyrights they own and, sometimes, are asked to transfer away.

OWNING COPYRIGHT

The fact that copyright applies automatically whenever original expression is fixed in tangible form does not mean that there are no issues or potential sources of dispute about that ownership. Two areas in which the ownership of scholarly works can come into dispute are "joint authorship" and "works made for hire." The first of these issues is actually relatively straightforward, although the rules may seem counterintuitive, and it can be addressed quite easily. The second issue, work for hire, is, unfortunately, complex and subject to a great deal of uncertainty. In both these situations, we must start with the fundamental principle that the initial owner of every copyright is the "author" of the fixed and original expression and then proceed to the vexed question of who is an author.

Joint Authorship

Many works of scholarship are the product of collaborations between a number of different people, but not all of those collaborators are joint authors in the legal sense. The definition of a joint author is one who makes a contribution of original expression to a work with the intention that that contribution be "merged into inseparable or interdependent parts of a unitary whole" (see 17 U.S.C. § 101 under "joint work"). To fully understand this concept, we need to briefly unpack three parts of the definition—the idea of authorship itself, the required intention, and the notion of a "unitary whole."

The Copyright Act actually does not define an "author" directly, but it does tell us that copyright attaches to "original works of authorship." In a 1991 case, the United States Supreme Court decided that this phrase meant that some modicum of creativity, not merely hard work, was required to get a copyright. In *Feist Publications v. Rural Telephone Service*, which was already mentioned in chapter 2, the court was asked to decide if copying of a phone book by a rival company constituted copyright infringement (499 U.S. 340 (1991)). Justice O'Connor, writing for the majority, held that even though a great deal of labor went into assembling the original phone book (the court used the phrase "sweat of the brow"), there was not sufficient creativity in the assemblage of facts to warrant copyright protection; the phone book, in short, was not a "work of authorship." From this case and others, we can infer that a potential joint author must contribute some minimal level of original expression eligible in itself for copyright protection.

This requirement has consequences for scholarly works, especially for journal articles, where persons are sometimes listed as authors even though their contribution was merely a matter of support rather than actual original expression. It is not uncommon, for example, for the principal investigator on a grant to be listed as an author even when he or she has had no role in writing the article other than securing the funding and overseeing the research that supported it. This kind of "courtesy" authorship does not create authorship in the copyright sense, and people listed as authors for this kind of reason are not joint authors. Only those who contribute original expression can be joint authors.

Another requirement of joint authorship is intent, and another case helps us illustrate what is required. In *Larson v. Thompson*, a dramaturge who was hired to help clarify the storyline and improve the script of the musical *Rent* before it went to Broadway claimed she was a joint author of the production (147 F.3d 195 (2d Cir. 1998)). Although Jonathan Larson, the principal author, had tragically died on the night of the final dress rehearsal, the Second Circuit Court of Appeals looked at "factual indicia" to find that there was not a "mutual intent" that would create joint authorship. The court was very explicit that "the contribution even of significant language to a work does not automatically suffice to confer co-author status on the contributor" (Thompson, 147 F.3d at 202). So for academic authors, the general lesson is that joint authorship is never a matter of accident or surprise; to create a situation where different authors hold copyright jointly, they must have intended to combine their contributions into a finished product.

The final requirement, for a "unitary whole," is not difficult to understand. The contributions must be inseparable, as when several people all contribute sections of a journal article that cannot be divided or distinguished in any practical way, or interdependent, as when a lyricist and a composer each contribute different parts to a song. An academic example might be an instructional video in which one professor created the visuals while another contributed the voiced-over lecture.

Once we have determined that a scholarly work is a product of joint authorship, we might well ask why it matters. The answer is that each joint author owns an equal and undivided interest in the copyright. This means that any joint author can exercise each of the exclusive rights, subject to an obligation to account to the other joint authors for any profits. Specifically, a single joint author can authorize publication and otherwise license the unified work for various purposes; that author does not need the permission of the others. The "equal and undivided" interest that each joint author holds in the copyright is not dependent on the amount of original expression each contributed; once a group of contributors have met the requirements of joint authorship, they have equal interests regardless of the size or importance of their contributions.

Research Example—Joint Authorship

The kind of conflict that can arise over joint authorship is nicely illustrated by a real academic dispute that arose regarding a journal article written by three researchers. Perhaps surprisingly, the issue that gave rise to a lawsuit was the order in which the names of the three authors were listed on an article describing a clinical training program for pharmacists. An untenured professor named Weinstein asserted that he had done the majority of the work on both the program and the article, so his name should have been first, rather than last, as it was when the article was published. In order to raise a cognizable claim, however, Weinstein asserted that the revision and publication of the article without his consent was copyright infringement. The Seventh Circuit Court of Appeals rejected this claim, based on the understanding of the rights of joint authors explained above; the court held that each author named on the article was a co-owner of the copyright and each was entitled to make revisions and authorize publication without consulting the others (Weinstein v. University of Illinois, 811 F.2d 1091 (1981))

The lesson from the *Weinstein* case discussed in this research example is that it is very important to have an understanding with collaborators in advance and to work out expectations about revisions, credit, and publication before they result in disagreements and, possibly, litigation. Understanding the scope of rights that each joint author exercises independently of the others provides a strong motivation for clear and frank discussions that anticipate potential disputes and avert them.

Work Made for Hire

The case of *Weinstein v. University of Illinois* also raises another, more troubling prospect about academic scholarship, the question of whether a scholarly work might be considered a work made for hire under the Copyright Act. If it is, such a work would be owned not by the faculty members who create it but by the institutions that employ them. The lower court in *Weinstein* had dismissed his complaint because it said he had no right to bring the complaint since the university, not Professor Weinstein, was the owner of the article under the work for hire provision of our copyright law. As we will see, the appellate court rejected this idea based on an old common law doctrine of dubious application. Nevertheless, the possibility that universities rather than individual scholars own academic copyrights is a persistent notion that regularly troubles faculty authors. Indeed, the appellate court in *Weinstein* even admitted that the statutory language defining work for hire "is general enough to make every academic article a 'work for hire' and therefore vest exclusive control in universities rather than scholars" (Weinstein, 811 F.2d at 1095).

The statutory language in question certainly seems unequivocal; a work is designated work made for hire whenever it is "prepared by an employee within the scope of his or her employment."[2] The effect of this definition is that such works are owned by the employers from the moment of creation; the ownership provisions of the Copyright Act clearly tell us that the employer is considered the author of a work made for hire (17 U.S.C. § 201(b)). Since authors are the initial owners of every copyright, there is no need for an employee to transfer his or her work done as part of the employment to the employer; the employer already owns it unless "the parties have expressly agreed otherwise in a written instrument signed by them" (17 U.S.C. § 201(b)).

There is a further definition in the work for hire provisions that, although less applicable for most scholars, may be significant for adjunct professors and grant recipients. This part of the definition deals with works created by independent contractors, people who are hired to do a specific job but are not regular employees.[3] This provision refutes the popular belief that if one pays for a work to be created, one automatically is the owner of that work. In fact, it is rather difficult for the copyright in a commissioned work to belong to the party that commissioned it. For the work of an independent contractor to be considered a work made for hire, it must first fall into one of nine categories enumerated in the law, and it must be the subject of a written agreement that explicitly states that the work will be a work for hire. In an important Supreme Court case called *Center for Creative Non-Violence v. Reid* (490 U.S. 730 (1989)), an

---

2.   17 U.S.C. § 101, definition of "work made for hire." Note that determining who is an employee or an employer can also be a complex matter in some situations, but in the case of, at least, full-time salaried faculty, there is little doubt that they are employees, in the legal sense, of their universities.

3.   The distinction between a regular employee and an independent contractor is determined by a number of factors, including who provides the materials for the work, who sets the work schedule, who controls decisions about the working process, and perhaps most importantly, how the payments are treated for tax purposes.

organization that commissioned a sculpture was found to own the physical object but not the copyright and was therefore prevented from making a copy of the artwork for touring purposes. The court found that Mr. Reid, the artist, was an independent contractor and that the agreement between the parties did not include a provision stating that the sculpture would be a work for hire. If a commissioned work is not a work made for hire, the actual artist or creator holds the initial copyright in the work, and not the commissioning party. Of course, if the parties decide later to transfer copyright in the work from the contractor to the commissioning party, they may do so by agreement. Work for hire determines only the initial owner of copyright; it does not inhibit later transfers in any way.

Research Example—Work Made for Hire

The present author is an administrative employee of a major university. As such, the works I produce as part of my regular job, which often consist of issue briefings for other administrators and legal opinion letters on intellectual property matters for faculty members, are almost certainly work made for hire under US law and are therefore owned by my employer. This book, on the other hand, is not written within the scope of my employment, so the copyright would normally belong to me. I am not, of course, a regular employee of the Association of College and Research Libraries. Furthermore, the payment of royalties, and even of an advance against those royalties, does not make the book a work for hire under the independent contractor provisions of the copyright law. The copyright might, ultimately, belong to the ACRL but only if I, as the original copyright holder, transfer those rights to the Association as part of our agreement for publication.

If these provisions were applied as they stand to academic scholarship created by regular faculty members at universities and colleges, those works would mostly have to be considered works made for hire. In that case, the universities and colleges would own all of the copyrights. But such a conclusion would overturn literally centuries of tradition in academia, and it would create havoc with publications, since it would require extensive analysis to be sure, in each case, who has the right to authorize publication and to transfer rights as necessary. Two mechanisms are at work to prevent this chaotic situation—a common law tradition against applying work for hire provisions to academics (sometimes called the "teacher exception") and university policies that usually disclaim any claim to copyright in, at least, the traditional scholarly works of faculty members. We will now examine each of these attempts to avoid the work for hire provisions in academia; it may be surprising to discover what weak supports for individual copyright ownership each provides.

Work Made for Hire—The Common Law "Teacher Exception"

To understand the teacher exception, we first must realize that work for hire itself was originally common law—judge-made rules formulated in the course of deciding specific cases. At the turn of the twentieth century, courts (including the Supreme Court) began to realize that, as a matter of fairness, employers should own copyright in certain works that were created at their expense and for their business purposes.[4] The doctrine of work made for hire was first codified in the copyright law when the law was thoroughly revised in 1909, but the doctrine was really just mentioned in passing; it was not defined, and courts continued to interpret it under principles of common law equity.

It did not take long for those principles to require judges to distinguish between situations where work for hire should apply and those where its application might work an injustice. The teacher exception, which was

4. Representative cases include Bleistein v. Donaldson Lithographing Co. in the Supreme Court, 188 U.S. 239 (1903), and Colliery Engineering Co. v. United Correspondence Schools, 94 F. 152 (S.D.N.Y. 1899).

first articulated in 1929, was one such attempt to make distinctions in the name of fairness. In that year, two men, one of them an instructor at the US Army Officer School at Ft. Leavenworth, wrote two separate books about sketching and reading maps. Mr. Sherrill, the Army instructor, accused the other author, named Graves, of copyright infringement, and Graves defended himself by claiming, in part, that Sherrill was not the copyright owner in the original book because it was written while Sherrill was an employee of the federal government (57 Wash. L.R. 286 (D.C. 1929)). Graves claimed, in short, that Sherrill's book was a work made for hire. The court rejected this defense, holding that "the court does not know of any authority holding that a professor is obligated to reduce his lectures to writing or if he does so that they become the property of the institution employing him" (57 Wash. L.R. at 297). This case is paradigmatic for the teacher exception to work for hire in two ways. First, it relies on the belief that writing and publication are not explicit requirements in the employment of professors. Second, it arises in a situation where a third party is charged with infringement and defends by claiming that the aggrieved professor does not own his own copyright; in this situation, the interests of the employing university and the employed faculty member are not adverse, they are both interested in punishing the third-party infringer.

Another case decided under the 1909 Copyright Act illustrates even more clearly how the teacher exception was usually applied in situations where the institution and the teacher were on the same side. *Williams v. Weisser*, decided in 1969 (78 Cal. Rptr. 542 (Cal. Ct. App. 1969)), has a rather modern feeling to it, since it reflects controversial practices that have accelerated in the Internet age. Weisser was an enterprising gentleman who conceived of the idea of publishing outline versions of popular courses taught at UCLA. To that end, he hired students to attend classes, including the anthropology class of Professor Williams, and take careful notes intended for subsequent publication. When Williams brought suit against Weisser for copyright infringement, UCLA's vice chancellor testified on his behalf, clearly demonstrating that the university's interests lay in a finding that professors owned the copyright in their lectures. Again, there was no direct conflict between faulty member and employer in this case; both were aligned against a third-party infringer.

The *Williams* court gave three reasons for its finding that notes in his lectures belong to Williams rather than to UCLA. First, and we have seen this before, it pointed out that professors were hired to teach but that "no particular method or expression is prescribed to accomplish that purpose" (78 Cal. Rptr. at 546). Second, the court thought that giving ownership to faculty was a better way to deal with the "peripatetic" nature of professors, since it avoided complications when instructors moved from one institution to another. Finally, the court turned this reasoning around to hold that the alternative, where universities would own works as work made for hire, would also be problematic for the universities themselves, since it would complicate hiring a professor away from a rival institution. Thus the court concluded that the work made for hire doctrine should not be "blindly applied" to the situation of a teacher giving lectures in his or her classroom (78 Cal. Rprt. at 547).

Both of these cases were decided while the 1909 Copyright Act was in effect. When the act was radically revised in 1976, the work made for hire doctrine was defined much more explicitly in the law, as has been described above. One question that was not answered at that time, and has not been clearly answered in the decades since, is whether or not the teacher exception remains viable under the new copyright regime; several legal scholars have suggested that the new rigor in defining work for hire does not leave room for a flexible exception based on equity (see, e.g., Dreyfuss 1987; Simon 1982–83). Courts have not offered definitive guidance, but the trend seems to be against a continuing teacher exception, especially when the dispute over ownership is directly between the university employer and the faculty employee.

On the one hand, in the *Weinstein* case and in another case (Hays v. Sony Corp. of America, 847 F. 2d 412 (7th Cir. 1988)) in the Seventh Circuit Court of Appeals, judges expressed the opinion that the teacher exception might, or at least should, persist after the adoption of the 1976

Copyright Act. In both cases the judges were commenting on a matter that they did not have to decide to rule in the cases, and their opinions therefore did not become binding precedents. On the other hand, the one case that squarely presented a dispute between a university and its faculty employee over who owned the copyright in classroom material came down in favor of work made for hire. In *Vanderhurst v. Colorado Mountain College District*, the facts presented exactly that situation, which had not arisen before in academic work for hire conflicts: a dispute directly between the faculty member and his employer (16 F. Supp. 2d 1297 (C. Colo. 1998)).

Vanderhurst argued that his copyright in the course outlines for his veterinary technology class were infringed when the college continued to use the outlines after Vanderhurst himself had been dismissed. The court treated this purely as a matter of applying the work for hire doctrine and did not mention the teacher exception at all. In determining the scope of Vanderhurst's employment, the court applied much broader reasoning than was used in the earlier *Sherrill v. Graves* case, finding that even though Vanderhurst used his own time and materials, the outlines were "one method of carrying out the objectives of his employment" and were "directly connected with the work for which he was employed" (16 F. Supp 2d at 1407). On this basis, the court granted a summary judgment for the college on the issue of copyright ownership.

Work for Hire and New Forms of Scholarship

This quick review of the teacher exception to the work made for hire doctrine suggests that there is probably still no problem regarding faculty ownership of traditional works of scholarship, including journal articles and monographs. The reasons given for the teacher exception continue to apply to these materials, and universities have very little incentive to challenge ownership by faculty authors. But the *Vanderhurst* case suggests that teaching materials, and by extension new kinds of materials created in the Internet age, present much more doubtful situations. In an age when nearly every class has an online component and a large part of teaching preparation involves creating presentations and handouts intended for Internet distribution, many more faculty creations have value apart from the work of an individual faculty member. Colleges may wish to exploit successful online teaching materials even after the faculty member who created them is no longer teaching the course or even has left the institution. In that situation, the circumstances are very different from those in which the teacher exception arose and look much more like *Vanderhurst*.

In addition, new forms of digital scholarship such as data mapping projects, visualizations, and digital reconstructions of historical material culture also do not fit the traditional models of scholarship. They often are not independent of specialized equipment owned by the employing institution, and sometimes they can have publicity value for the college or university. Faculty who create these kinds of works cannot rely on the teacher exception anymore than those who create online teaching resources can. In both cases, the determination of who owns the copyright in the work in question will be either a matter of institutional policy or a specifically negotiated agreement.

Teaching Example—Work Made for Hire

Faculty members today often create a variety of online materials for each class they teach. Presentations that were given in a face-to-face classroom usually also end up in an online course management environment. Sometimes special outlines are also created for that environment in order to facilitate student studying. Collections of images, music, and video clips may also be incorporated. These collections often are valuable to the university apart from any specific instructor, and retaining copyright in them can save a good deal of money when another instructor takes over the class. The faculty author may also want to keep this material for use at a subsequent employer. The teacher exception will not necessarily provide a solution to this potential conflict. Often university IP policies do address these situations, and when they do not, they should be revised. It is important to remember that the decision about ownership is only half of the task in creating a successful IP policy; it is also necessary to designate use rights—groups or institutions that have a predetermined license to use a work even if ownership is directed elsewhere. Thus a faculty author may retain ownership in her online course materials, and the university can also hold a license to continue to use the materials even after the professor leaves for another university.

UNIVERSITY IP POLICIES

Because of the confusion and administrative burden that could result if a college or university actually tried to assert work for hire over all faculty-authored creations, many institutions have adopted policies attempting to vary the outcome of these analyses. Most copyright ownership policies in higher education disclaim any intention of asserting work for hire over, at least, traditional works of faculty scholarship. Usually these policies are part of the faculty handbook or are otherwise incorporated into the terms of a faculty member's employment.

While these policies are certainly adopted in good faith and attempts to circumvent them are exceedingly rare, it must be noted that there is some doubt about whether or not a policy enacted in this way would really prevent an institution from asserting copyright ownership in the rare situation in which a scholarly work proved to be valuable enough to make a breach of such policy worthwhile. The reason for this doubt is that the "work for hire" provisions of the Copyright Act specify that a work that would otherwise be made for hire can be taken out of that category only if "the parties have expressly agreed otherwise in a written instrument signed by them" (17 U.S.C. § 201(b)). Some scholars have speculated over whether, if a direct conflict arose, a policy document that was merely incorporated by reference into the employment contract of faculty members would be sufficient to meet this statutory requirement (see, e.g., Dreyfuss 1987; Packard 2002). Nevertheless, in most situations the policy of an institution will be the most relevant guide to copyright ownership questions. If institutions have such a policy, it is important for faculty scholars to know what it says. If institutions do not have a policy, drafting one is an excellent way to reduce the risk of conflict with faculty or publishers in the future.

For faculty inventors, it is even more important to know the contents of an institutional patent policy. These documents are often referred to by the title "Technology Transfer." Unlike copyright policies, technology transfer documents usually assert that the institution has some share in patents that result from work done in its labs and by its employees. We have already detailed the reason for these different policy approaches, so all that remains is to consider the specific provisions that the various IP policies at an institution may include.

Copyright Policies

The norm for college and university copyright policies is, as has already been stated, to cede ownership to the faculty author. Because authors are nearly always the ones who work with publishers and ultimately sign publication agreements, this arrangement is sensible and avoids needless bureaucracy. But such policies are nearly always subject to exceptions for specific types of works or other situations in which the university does assert ownership. Exceptions to the norm of faculty ownership typically include administrative works, software developed for utilitarian rather than research purposes, and some classroom material. In regard to this last category, there is an interesting debate going on about who owns the recordings of classroom lectures and discussions, which are becoming quite common. As "classroom capture" increases, the use of those record-ings outside of the bounds of the specific class, where they are useful for student review, raises the issue of whether faculty, and even student, permission is needed before an institution makes such material public.

In many situations, the most important element of a campus copyright policy is not the ownership decisions that it memorializes but the use rights that it creates. Often policies will say that faculty own all rights in specified categories of work but also create a perpetual license for the institution to use those works. Likewise a policy could assert institutional ownership over works created by administrative staff but also give to those staff members a perpetual right to use the works they created for other professional activities. Often these use rights are the key to avoiding conflict over ownership issues. To return to the issue of classroom capture, we can see how various policy elements, including ownership decisions and use rights, can interact to promote a fair and conflict-free environment. In all likelihood the faculty author will be the owner of her lecture notes and, by extension, of a recording made of her lecture. A good policy should include the professor's right to authorize recording and to prevent specific lectures from being captured if she feels that is necessary. But the policy can also stipulate that the institution has a continuing right to use such recordings as are made, usually for specified purposes, regardless of whether or not the instructor continues to be employed by that institution.

Teaching Example—The Rise of MOOCs

Eastern Pacific University has recently begun to offer massive open online courses in partnership with a commercial start-up company. Although EPU is excited to extend its global reach and offer classes to hundreds of thousands of students around the world, its faculty is concerned about who will own and have control over the materials created for these courses. One worry is that once all of the lectures are "in the can," the faculty creator will no longer be needed and the university, or the company , can offer the course without his or her participation.

EPU's copyright policy says that faculty members own the IP rights in their classroom materials, but that a license is automatically granted to the university and its students to use those materials. In discussions with its faculty, EPU decides that it wants this principle to also apply to MOOCs. The university determines that it would be unacceptable to most faculty for EPU to own the courseware, but that the license granted to the university must be better defined to account for these new opportunities and complexities.

Ultimately, the new license that is agreed upon makes a couple of significant additions to EPU's copyright policy. First, arrangements for revenue sharing are specified to account for the need of the university to recover costs from the creation of the MOOC and then to share any revenue generated with the faculty creator(s).

Also, a provision is inserted to specify that the faculty creator must approve anytime the course is to be reoffered. Finally, a complementary "conflict of interest" provision specifies that if the faculty member wants to reoffer the course on a different platform or with a different university, he or she must get permission from EPU to do so.

In the process of negotiating this policy revision, both EPU and its faculty came to understand that the issue of ownership is only part of the discussion, and perhaps not the most important part. What really matters is determining the interests of each party in use and reuse and negotiating a fair agreement that accounts for those interests through a license or series of licenses.

When constructing a copyright ownership policy, the first step is to identify all of the parties who may create copyright-protected content on campus. At a minimum, this will include faculty, administrators, other staff, and students. Different types of content should also be distinguished, including traditional scholarly works, administrative materials, classroom content, online courses, and so forth. Then ownership decisions can be made based on the type of work and the category into which the creator falls. Finally, decisions about the use rights that may be reserved for the other groups—those that do not own the copyright in a specific type of work—can be made and specified. Thus a faculty author will likely retain ownership in his scholarly works and no other group will have use rights. On the other hand, ownership of administrative materials created by the same faculty member may be vested in the university, while the faculty author would retain the right to use the material for specified professional purposes.

When creating the kind of policy matrix described above, detailing the ownership and use rights of different interested parties over different kinds of copyrightable works, it is important to recognize that students actually have an interest in such policies as well. In the ordinary situation, an institution will have no grounds for asserting ownership over student-created works. The fact that a paper is written for a college course, for example, does not give either the institution or the instructor a copyright interest. This is true even when the instructor has significant input into the idea for, and structure of, the work, as is often the case with theses and dissertations, since copyright does not protect ideas, only the expression of ideas. Nevertheless, students do have an interest in using certain works created at an institution, and policy documents ought to take that interest into account. For example, when a lecture is recorded for distribution through a learning management system, or a faculty presentation is made available in that way, students should know how they can and cannot use that material. Likewise, student notes are arguably a derivative work based on the intellectual property of the instructor—her lecture—and the scope of students' use rights need to be specified in order to address the "note selling" situations that have arisen occasionally for years and that are multiplying in this age of Internet distribution.

Research Example—Policy Application

In a conflict that took place at a US research university, an administrative employee in a research center was assigned to develop a curriculum to help teach the topic of the center's research to students in local secondary schools. The curriculum was quite successful, but a disagreement developed over its ownership when a new director for the center was appointed. The university's policy seemed to indicate that the employee author owned the copyright, and the new director was concerned about being able to continue to use and modify the curriculum if and when the employee left his position. Here the distinction between ownership and use proved very significant; the employee author was primarily interested in having his ownership acknowledged, while the center's director wanted to ensure continuing use rights. These things were not at all incompatible, and negotiation between the two parties yielded an agreement satisfactory to both sides. These negotiations would have been significantly easier if the institutional copyright policy had been more explicit about the use rights that were granted (and it is possible to question the wisdom of ceding the original ownership in this type of material to an administrative employee). But in the long run, the ownership issue was only a small part of the discussion, and a careful approach to how use rights were divided up, whether in a policy document or in direct negotiation, was the key to a successful resolution.

Patent Policies

University policy regarding patent ownership, which are often called "technology transfer" policies, tend to be more complex than copyright ownership policies. One reason for this is that they are heavily governed by federal law and by contractual provisions that govern grant monies. Complexity also results from the need to deal with a variety of circumstances impacting how cost of the patent application process will be borne and how profits from licensing of patented inventions will be shared. Two elements that are common to nearly all technology transfer policies, a disclosure requirement and guidelines regarding substantial use of institutional resources, will be the focus of our discussion here.

The most important provision of federal law that governs patents on campus is the Bayh–Dole Act of 1980.[5] Prior to that legislation, the presumption was that any patentable invention that arose from government-funded research was owned by the government. Bayh–Dole reversed this presumption, giving institutions the right to elect to retain title to such inventions, in the interests of encouraging entrepreneurship and streamlining the path to market for new discoveries.[6] Since most of the major research undertakings that result in patentable inventions on campus require significant funding from the government, this change has had a profound effect on faculty IP. Note that it is the institution, not the inventor, that is allowed to retain title. Since patent applications must be made in the name of the inventor, however, this provision forces institutions and their faculty researchers to work in close concert. Other provisions of Bayh–Dole require that the institution[7] disclose to the funding agency all inventions made in the course of funded research (or risk losing the title), mandate that royalties from any licensing of the invention be shared with the inventor, and regulate how universities may license the invention to commercial entities.[8]

---

5.   This law is formally titled "The University and Small Business Patent Procedures Act" and is codified at 35 U.S.C. §§ 200–212.

6.   A recent report on the effectiveness of Bayh–Dole concluded that the system it put in place has been largely successful at meeting these goals and recommended only minor adjustments. See Lederman 2010.

7.   Bayh–Dole applies not only to educational institutions but also to small businesses that receive federal research funding.

8.   Under Bayh–Dole, the government itself always holds a perpetual non-exclusive license to discoveries made in the course of funded research.

The requirement that inventions be disclosed to funders is one, but not the only, reason that almost all technology transfer policies include a mechanism for early notification of the institution whenever a researcher thinks she has discovered something patentable. This is important because disclosure to the government may be required even if the research is not directly funded by a federal grant if the research involved using equipment, personnel, or laboratory space that was itself financed through a grant. And even in the rare case where no federal funding is implicated, disclosure to the university is sensible because of the need for advice about maintaining the patentability of an invention (avoiding, for example, publications that would destroy the required "novelty") and because financial support in the patent application process, which can cost upwards of $30,000, is almost always necessary.[9]

The ownership of patentable inventions and the division of royalties between inventor and institution are often governed by formulas that are based on "significant use of university funds or facilities" (Duke University 2008). By designating significant use of *either* funds or facilities as triggers for an institutional interest in an invention, the provisions of Bayh–Dole are incorporated into such policies, but the policies often also use this criterion as a formula for dividing up any licensing royalties that an invention generates. Thus a new discovery in a biomedical lab that is licensed to a pharmaceutical company, for example, may generate substantial income.[10] Many policies will determine how this income will be split between inventor and university based on the size of the institutional investment. At the extreme end, a discovery made entirely by the researcher on her own time and with her own resources will be wholly owned by the inventor. On the other hand, where most of the research is

---

9. For more detail on these issues, see chapter 2.

10. In Stanford University v. Roche Molecular Systems (563 U.S. ___ (2011), docket no. 09-1159) the Supreme Court complicated the rules about university patents somewhat, in a situation where pharmaceutical profits were at stake. Basically, the court held that Stanford's policy language, under which a faculty inventor "agrees to assign" the IP rights, was trumped by an agreement with a commercial entity, through which the inventor "hereby [did] assign" those same rights.

done on university time and in a university lab, the university will usually own the invention, and there are often complex and sliding scales of how the monies will be distributed.

Before we complete our discussion of patents, we should acknowledge one more wrinkle in the ownership of inventions developed by a university employee, which is called a "shop right." The shop right is a patent equivalent to copyright's work made for hire doctrine. In the patent arena, it has not been codified in federal law but has developed in court actions.[11] Nevertheless, this "common law" shop right is well recognized; even in situations where there is no policy that governs ownership of inventions created by an employee—perhaps something invented in a lab at a small institution that seldom receives federal research grants—the employer institution is likely to have an "implied license" in the invention based on the shop right. Just as with the use rights we discussed as part of copyright policies, the shop right gives to the employer a license to use a patented invention even while that patent is owned by the individual inventor. This license for use is implied by law and is non-exclusive; it does not prevent the inventor from selling licenses to others, although it may slightly reduce the value of those licenses. Usually the shop right is overridden by technology transfer policies, just as work for hire rules are overridden by copyright policies at universities. But shop right doctrine could occasionally come into play in higher education research settings, as indicated above. And it is also the case that policy documents sometimes use the language of shop right when they designate non-exclusive use rights, occasionally even in the copyright context.

Trademark Policies

Even though trademarks—the name, logo, and mascot of an institution, for example—often generate substantial revenues for an institution, the

---

11. A very brief blog post (Falcon 2009) explains this shop right and cites the relevant court cases.

policies on trademark use normally have little effect on faculty members in their ordinary working lives. The situations in which a faculty member is most likely to use the institution's name are when he identifies himself, perhaps in an author's byline or a conference program, as a professor at, for example, the Ohio State University. This is always a permitted use of the trademark because it is an accurate identification of the author's affiliation and because it is used in an obviously noncommercial way. The situation in which a conflict might arise, however, is when a faculty member runs a business on the side. In that context, referring to her employment at a university might mislead people into believing that the university was endorsing the business. These kinds of uses are usually forbidden, or at least subject to an approval process, by the institution's trademark policies or conflict of interest rules. Whenever a "use in commerce" is made of an institutional trademark, even by a legitimate employee of the institution, the university must be mindful to avoid a false message of endorsement as well as the potential that the mark might be "diluted" by the use in question. If a faculty member has doubts about a particular use of the institution's name, it is well to consult a trademark policy or talk with the office charged with licensing the mark.[12]

CONCLUSION

The rules discussed above regarding ownership of copyrights, patents, and trademarks must be understood as default rules; they come into play in the absence of specific agreements between the parties. These default rules can almost always be changed by such specific agreements. University policies that are incorporated in the terms of faculty employment are one type of agreement that varies the conditions of IP ownership. On an even more granular level, these default rules and any local policies can

---

12. It is often the case that this office will be affiliated with the university stores, since they sell a great deal of trademarked and licensed merchandise.

be changed by negotiated agreements between the parties. Thus the best advice that can be given to faculty members who are creating intellectual property is to think ahead, especially if the form of that creation seems unusual or outside of the types of situations contemplated by any policies that are in place. If a potential author or inventor wants to be sure in advance of how ownership will be handled, she should contact the institution and negotiate an agreement that governs the particular situation. As long as these agreements do not contravene prior legal obligations (such as those undertaken with funding agencies), they will usually be enforceable and can provide some certainty about the situation so that both parties will know how to proceed.

When all of the copyright, patent, and trademark ownership questions have been settled, whether by law, policy, or negotiated agreement, one fundamental issue still remains. What is the purpose of IP ownership in higher education? The academic world is largely a gift economy, especially in regard to copyrighted works. These traditional products of scholarship seldom make any money for either the author or the institution; they are created and disseminated for the increase of knowledge and to further the academic reputation of the author. As we look further at how IP functions in academia and where it fails, it is well to keep in mind the fundamental question of what interests are served by IP ownership and how academic practices can best serve the interests that are most important to scholarship.

Using Copyrighted Works in Scholarship

DETERMINING AND managing the ownership of copyrights can be extremely significant for scholars. Nevertheless, the activity that occurs most frequently on university campuses and that has the most potential for creating disputes is the use in teaching and scholarship of copyrighted works owned by others. When the roles of scholars as both copyright owners and users of copyrighted works owned by others are balanced, it becomes easier to understand both the scholarly interests that are served, and those that are not served, by our copyright laws. While academics can often be very protective of the rights they own, they also understand the need to make some use of works owned by others in order to teach effectively and to continue the cumulative process of scholarship. When these activities are inhibited by the relatively opaque exceptions to copyright and its very long term, as they often are, it is easy to see that ownership over intellectual property is only half of what scholars need. As we now turn to examine how academics can and cannot use the copyrighted works of others in their professional labors, we will gain a better perspective on the interests that are most important in a balanced view of scholarship.

When considering any particular use of works that are owned by someone else, something which happens on a daily basis in the lives of most scholars, there are five questions that putative user should ask:[1]

1. Is the work I want to use subject to copyright protection?
2. Is there a license in place that governs my proposed use?
3. Is there a specific exception in the copyright law that allows my proposed use?
4. Is my proposed use a "fair use"?
5. Who should I ask for permission?

Thinking through these questions in this order will usually allow that user to avoid missing any necessary considerations and arrive at a sound judgment about the use. Even when all of these questions are carefully considered, however, it is necessary to recognize that the copyright law often does not offer clear-cut lines or definitive answers. Especially in the realm of fair use, which is the single copyright exception most relied upon by scholars, decisions are always a matter of good faith and reasonable analysis of risk. It is precisely in thinking about fair use that it is most helpful for scholars to look at their own interests as copyright holders and consider how they would want others to treat their own works as they consider using the works of others. But before we discuss fair use we should start at the beginning of our list of five questions.

---

1.   These five questions are found frequently in training materials on copyright , especially for academia. One excellent example of their use in such a tutorial is at the University of North Carolina, Charlotte, on the following website: http://copyright. uncc.edu/copyright/teaching/fivesteps.

IS THE WORK I WANT TO USE SUBJECT TO COPYRIGHT PROTECTION?

This question is the obverse of the question "Is the work I wish to use in the public domain?" It is important to realize that the public domain refers to the copyright status of a work and its availability for reuse. It is not the same as saying that a work is publicly available; many works that can be purchased in stores or located on the Internet are not in the public domain, even though they are accessible to the public.

The Center for the Study of the Public Domain at Duke University Law School offers this definition of the public domain: "the realm of material—ideas, images, sounds, discoveries, facts, texts—that is unprotected by intellectual property rights and free for all to use or build upon" (Duke Law 2010). The key here is that a work that is in the public domain is free for anyone to use, reuse, alter, or adapt. If a work at issue is in the public domain, the copyright analysis can stop and the putative user can proceed to do whatever she wants with the work. Thus the discovery that a work is in the public domain is very liberating and empowering. Unfortunately, it can sometimes be very difficult to determine with any certainty that a particular work is, in fact, in the public domain.

There are four large categories of works that have entered the public domain: (1) works in which the copyright protection has expired, (2) works that failed to comply with formalities such as registration during the period when these were required, (3) works produced by US government employees, and (4) works that fail to meet the minimum "creativity" requirement of copyright law. The key here is to recognize that the focus is always on what the work is, who made it, and when was it made. The actual *availability* of the work has little to do with public domain status. Thus, works that are widely available on the Internet are not, absent other qualifying features, in the public domain. Each of these categories is discussed in more detail below.

Works Published before 1923

Any work published before 1923 is in the public domain in the United States. This is probably the only truly simple rule in copyright. If the work has been published and carries a publication or copyright date of 1922 or earlier, it is in the public domain and can be used without permission or the need to resort to any of the exceptions to copyright; there simply is no longer any copyright in the work.[2]

Even with this simple rule, however, there is the need to add an explanation and a caveat.

Often a work that was originally published prior to 1923 is republished thereafter. This situation can give rise to some confusion when a user wishes to reuse the earlier work, but has access only to the newer reprinting. The important explanation regarding this situation is that, once a work rises into the public domain, republication does not revive a copyright in that work. No matter how many republications of the works of Herman Melville take place, the copyright in *Moby Dick* has expired and will not be reawakened.

To this explanation must be added a caveat. Republications of a public domain work often include new material, usually in the form of an introduction, afterword, or explanatory notes. Even if the text itself is in the public domain, this additional material can be protected by copyright. Thus a professor who wishes to scan the entirety of *Moby Dick* and place it on a website for her students must be certain that the scan contains only Melville's text and not any of the scholarly apparatus added, for example, to the 1967 Norton critical edition.

---

2. The exact meaning of publication is, however, a potential complication to this rule. There is no consistent definition of publication and, while it may be relatively clear in regard to books, determining if an image or a song has been published, especially since performance and display do not necessarily equate to publication, can be quite difficult.

Teaching Example—Public Domain Works

Professor Johnson wants all of the students in his micro-economics course to read a thematic issue of the *American Economic Review* called "What Can a Man Afford?" This was supplement number 2 from the *AER* and was published in December 1921. Since the journal is still being published today, Professor Johnson is worried that the publisher will have a copyright claim and may be upset, even send a "cease and desist" letter, if he scans the entire issue and puts it up on a class website. But because this issue was published prior to 1923, Professor Johnson does not need to be concerned. Even assuming that it was published with notice and the copyright was renewed, as required by the law in effect at the time, protection expired at the end of 1977. This issue of the journal is in the public domain, and the professor is free to reproduce and distribute it as he sees fit.

Works Published in the United States between 1923 and 1963

For copyright to persist in a work published between 1923 and 1963, it is necessary that that work initially carried a copyright notice and that the copyright was renewed after an initial term of twenty-eight years. Although these formalities have been abolished in our current copyright law, works published in the United States during this forty-year span still must have complied with those rules or they are in the public domain. Thus a work published (with all the complexities attached to that concept) during that period that did not carry any notice of copyright immediately rose into the public domain.

While it is relatively rare to find works that were published during this period without any copyright notice, it is quite common that a work was published with the required notice—© plus a date and name—but for which the copyright was not renewed after the initial term of protection (twenty-eight years) expired. In a study of copyrights registered between 1935 and 1970, legal scholars concluded that less than 15 percent of the works registered for copyright had been renewed (Landes and Posner 2003, 242). Therefore a significant portion of the works published during the period between 1923 and 1963 are in the public domain due to lack of renewal.

Determining if a copyright was renewed during this period when renewal was required has become much easier since the records of the Copyright Office have been digitized and made available in a couple of different databases.[3] If one knows that a book was first published in the United States during this period and no renewal record can be found, it is fairly safe to assume that the work is in the public domain. Two qualifications must be added to this assurance, however.

First, this procedure should be relied upon only for books. The renewal records that make up these databases are not complete, and they are more comprehensive in regard to books than for other formats such as recordings.

Second, it is important to know that a work was published first in the United States and not published simultaneously in another country. Because of some technical amendments made to our copyright law in 1989, works that were published in another country, either originally or simultaneously with a US publication, and that rose into the public domain in the United States solely because of the failure to comply with the registration and renewal process, had their copyrights restored.[4] These works will not be in the public domain until 2019 at the earliest. This means that one must be quite certain that a book was published first (or

---

3. Stanford University Libraries maintains one such database at http://collections. stanford.edu/copyrightrenewals/bin/page?forward=home. Another database, designed by students and faculty at the Tulane Law School, that employs these records is the Durationator, found at www.durationator.com.

4. For purposes of this provision of the copyright law, *simultaneous* means within thirty days after the US publication.

exclusively) in the United States before making a search of the renewal records and assuming, when a renewal is not found, that the book is in the public domain. Translations are one type of work for which this provision is especially troublesome; if the US work is a translation of a work first published in another language, investigation must be done to establish if the original was published overseas in a manner that would lead to a restored copyright.[5]

Federal Government Works

The United States is a rarity among the nations of the world in denying copyright protection to the works of its federal government. While most other countries recognize some form of "Crown copyright," works created by the employees of the United States are automatically dedicated to the public domain, which makes a rich contribution to the set of materials freely available for scholarship.

The copyright act defines a work of the United States government as "a work prepared by an officer or employee of the United States Government as part of that person's official duties" (17 U.S.C. § 105). While this is a broad group of works on a variety of topics, two limitations must be recognized.

First, copyright protection is unavailable only for works of the federal government. Works created at the state and local level may still be subject to copyright. Some states and localities do claim rights in certain kinds of works, including building codes and maps. There is a long-standing judicial tradition, however, denying protection for local and state judicial decisions and statutory laws.

Second, some things that appear to be works of the federal government are, in fact, created by independent contractors who are not "officers or

---

5.   This wrinkle in the duration of copyright, which is an exception to the general rule that works do not come out of the public domain once they are within it, is carefully explained, with examples and a description of the research procedures that are needed, by Peter Hirtle (2008).

employees" of the United States. In these cases, the contractor likely will hold a copyright. One example here would be the photography in the colorful brochures handed out at national parks; usually these pictures are taken by contract photographers who could still claim copyright, even though the brochure is distributed by a government agency.

Research Example—Government Work

Professor Gordon is writing a book about insect infestations in the Midwest corn crop. She finds two government studies that each contain charts and tables that she would like to use to bolster her discussion. One study was prepared by a scientist working for the US Department of Agriculture, while the other is by an agent of the University of Nebraska, Lincoln Extension. Professor Gordon must account to her publisher for the right to incorporate all material that she did not create herself. The first study, because it was prepared by a federal employee, is in the public domain. The second study, however, may be subject to a copyright claim, since its author was a state employee. In this case, Professor Gordon must either have permission for her use or rely on fair use.

Works Lacking Minimal Creativity

In the famous decision, already discussed in previous chapters, called *Feist v. Rural Telephone*, the United States Supreme Court decided that some works, specifically the white pages of a telephone book, lack even the "modicum of creativity" that is necessary for copyright protection to attach to a work (499 U.S. 340 (1991)). The Copyright Act provides protection to "works of authorship" defined very broadly, but the court held that mere effort alone—"sweat of the brow" was the quaint phrase the court used—was not sufficient to create a work of authorship; a minimal level of creativity is required.

Generally all of the works that scholars encounter in the course of teaching and research are far more than minimally creative, so there will be no question that they are protectable under copyright. But there is one situation that often arises that is worth considering under this topic.

When a photographer takes a photo of a work of art, there are potentially two different copyrights involved, one held (initially) by the artist in the work that is photographed and one held by the photographer in her image of that work. But what if the artwork itself is in the public domain and the photographic image is simply an accurate reproduction of that artwork that adds nothing that is creative or expressive? That was the question addressed by a federal district court in a case called *Bridgeman Art Library v. Corel Corp.* (36 F.Supp2d 191 (S.D.N.Y. 1999)). In that case, the court found that color transparencies of artworks that were themselves in the public domain did not add sufficient creative expression, even the mere "modicum" demanded by the Supreme Court in *Feist*, to gain a copyright for the photographer. While most photographic work certainly is protected by copyright, this limited class of "bare" reproductions of two-dimensional public domain artworks are themselves free for use because they do not rise to the level of creativity necessary for copyright protection.[6]

Teaching Example—Photographic Reproduction

Professor Reynolds wants all of her students to closely examine the painting *The Kiss* by Gustave Klimt. She finds an excellent photographic reproduction of it published in a 2007 book. She is able to copy and distribute that reproduction to her students because the photo is in the public domain—it adds no creative expression to the public

---

6.   A photograph of a three-dimensional work such as a sculpture certainly does contain enough creative expression for protection.

domain artwork—and publication of the photo in a new publication does not create a copyright in incorporated material
that does not have protection on its own terms.

The Internet Is NOT the Public Domain

The previous four categories we discussed were all types of works that are
in the public domain and therefore free for anyone to use as they wish.
This brief section is added to reiterate that merely distributing a work to
the public, even the worldwide public that can access the Internet, does
not place a work in the public domain. This is not necessarily an obvious point; one occasionally hears publication on the Internet spoken of
as release into the public domain, which it is not. In fact, a well-known
French news agency recently reused photographs, without permission,
that it took from an Internet photo-sharing site, and defended itself—
unsuccessfully—by claiming that they were free for anyone to use by
virtue of Internet distribution.[7]

For material found on the Internet, the default assumption should be
that copyright protection applies unless either the work is obviously in
the public domain for one of the reasons described above or there is a
statement about rights that accompanies the material and permits the
contemplated use. Consider the following example.

Teaching Example—The Internet

A professor of physics wants his students to view a video
of the famous reaction caused by dropping Mentos into a
bottle of Coke. He can find many such videos on YouTube
and identifies three candidates. The first is produced by
the Discovery Channel and includes advertisements, the

---

7. The case is called Agence France Presse v. Morel and is described in Olivier
Laurent's (2010) article.

second is uploaded by a user and carries no statement of any kind about rights or reuse, and the third, also user-submitted, has a Creative Commons license. The professor must assume that both of the first two are protected by copyright, even though one is anonymous. His best option is to use the video with the Creative Commons license.

As the example makes clear, licensing is an important part of copyright decision making, especially on the Internet and in regard to other digital resources. For that reason, the next question to address, when and if it is determined that a work is protected by copyright, is whether or not a license applies that authorizes the proposed use.

IS THERE A LICENSE IN PLACE THAT GOVERNS MY PROPOSED USE?

Once it is determined that the work to be used is still protected by copy-right—which is to say it has not yet entered the public domain—the next question one should ask is if a license of any kind covers the desired use. A license is simply prior permission to exercise a right or perform an activity that the licensee would not otherwise be allowed to perform; my neighbor's permission for my children to cross her property in order to reach their school bus stop (which would otherwise be a trespass) is a simple type of license.

Most licenses are more formal than this type of bare permission. They are basically contracts between two parties, the rights holder and the putative user of the materials owned by that rights holder. Because they are private agreements between specific parties, courts have held that most kinds of rights granted by public laws, including copyrights, can be altered or waived by licenses as between those parties that agree to the license. Thus a user who is party to a license can agree not to make use of the exceptions provided in copyright law, such as fair use, in exchange for access to a work or set of works, while the rights holder agrees to allow certain specified uses in spite of his or her exclusive rights.

Not all licenses are formal documents. Libraries have such carefully negotiated agreements for most of the commercial databases they acquire, but many other licenses are much less formal, including the "click-through" terms of use that users agree to when they participate in online services like YouTube or Google Docs and the "shrink-wrap" licenses that accompany the purchase of a software package. In general, courts have held that these licenses are enforceable, even though the consumer often has no opportunity to negotiate the terms of the agreement.[8] Obviously, as more and more academic work, both research and teaching, comes to depend on online services, these licenses grow in importance for scholars.

We will look briefly at three types of licenses that impact scholarship—the commercial database license (regardless of its form), the blanket licenses that rights holders use to sell permission for certain uses to entire campuses, and the Creative Commons license, which is a popular mechanism by which rights holders can grant prior permission for certain uses of their work.

Commercial and Online Licenses

As has already been suggested, licenses for commercial products come in a variety of forms, from the formal contractual documents that govern the use of databases like JSTOR, Web of Science, or AP Images to the barely noticed twenty-six-page agreement that all users consent to when they sign on to iTunes. There is really very little to say about these particular licenses because they are all different and it is necessary to

---

8.   The most often cited case on the topic of the enforceability of these non-negotiable licenses, as well as on the issue of licenses superseding copyright law as to the parties who form the licensing contract, is ProCD Inc. v. Zeidenberg, 86 F.3d 1447, a 1996 case from the 7th Circuit Court of Appeals upholding the validity of a shrink-wrap license the was used to govern consumer use of CDs containing a set of phone books for the United States.

know the terms of each in order to know what uses for the content of that particular database are permitted.

To take one example, consider the photographs that are available in the AP Images database. This database offers a remarkable variety of current events and other worldwide photography that can be a rich source for illustrations and teaching materials. Whatever uses of these photographs might ordinarily be permitted under either the TEACH Act or fair use provisions of the copyright law are irrelevant once the license is signed; in the case of AP Images, several categories of uses, such as "educational" and "editorial," are defined, and those definitions circumscribe what campus users can do with the photos. In some cases these rules are more restrictive than what copyright alone would permit, and in some cases they are more generous. The point is that it is the license terms that govern permitted uses.

Blanket Licenses

Several organizations in the United States, called collective rights societies, represent hundreds or thousands of different rights holders in a particular field and license the right to use the works of those rights holders. The best known, perhaps, is ASCAP, the American Society of Composers and Publishers, which on behalf of its many members licenses the right to publicly perform musical compositions. If a local "cover" band wants to do its own version of Elton John's "Goodbye, Yellow Brick Road" at a local venue, it would get a license form ASCAP or it counterparts, called BMI and SESAC, for the right to do so. Of interest to scholars and teachers, these organizations each offers a blanket license for performances on college campuses of the music they represent. A university that purchases a license from all three societies can pretty much allow most musical performances on its campus; the licenses cover not only works performed by student groups and faculty ensembles, but even music played in elevators and while callers are on hold.

As with the database licenses, it is important to know the terms of these blanket performance licenses. In the case of ASCAP, BMI, and SESAC, it is necessary to know what composers and publishers are included in the catalog of each society so as to be sure that a particular performance is, in fact, covered by one of the licenses. One growing area of concern is exactly what the licenses permit in terms of recording and broadcast of performances that take place on college and university campuses. A student orchestra, for example, is almost certainly covered for its live performance of popular classical and modern works, but if that performance is recorded, can it be broadcast over the Web? The current version of these licenses on my campus permits such recording and rebroadcast over a university-owned website or cable TV station, but not through commercial venues. These provisions are likely to change as technology evolves, but the terms of the blanket licenses, whatever they are, will determine the scope of permissible activities.

An especially important type of licensing for academia is that available for textual material from the Copyright Clearance Center (CCC). The CCC sells individual licenses that are often purchased when a course pack or electronic reserve reading that exceeds the campus's understanding of fair use is offered to students. It also sells a blanket license, similar to those marketed by ASCAP et al., for such purposes, although it is important to recognize that not all publishers that work with the CCC to license reproduction rights also participate in its blanket license. Thus both types of licensing may be useful or necessary for a campus that provides lots readings to students through course pack collections or electronic reserves (either via the library or using individual course pages in a course management system).

Teaching Example—Course Content

Professor Durant wants to provide several resources to her students in addition to their textbook. She has several excerpts from books that she wants her students to read as supplemental material. Also, she has a recording of a performance by the campus orchestra of a piece that she wants her students to listen to. For the musical performance, she must look at the performance licenses held by the school. If they permit in-house rebroadcast (as most currently do) of performances of works in their catalogs, that portion of her course page should be all right. For the readings, she should first do a fair use analysis, using whatever guidance her campus provides for this purpose. If the readings exceed the understanding of fair use on her campus (it is, as we shall see, variable and hotly debated), she should inquire about whether the campus has a campus license from the CCC that covers the works in question, or she should seek individual permission through the CCC website (www.copyright.com).

Creative Commons Licenses

While most commercial licenses exist to restrict uses, often even more closely than copyright law alone would do, the Creative Commons is a licensing scheme designed to facilitate use, especially the noncommercial educational uses that we are concerned with here. If it is possible to locate the teaching or research resource one needs under a Creative Commons license, that resource will be available for use because the license will provide prior permission; in most cases there will be no need to ask anyone or look beyond the relatively simple terms of the CC license.[9]

The Creative Commons licenses were developed with creative artists in mind and are intended to facilitate Internet distribution.[10] Thus they are most useful for finding images, music, and video that can be

---

9. The Creative Commons licenses that authorize free use are commonly called CC licenses, which must be distinguished from the rather expensive individual and blanket licenses available from the CCC (Copyright Clearance Center).

10. The licensing scheme is explained at http://creativecommons.org. From that site it is also possible to craft a specific license and attach it to one's own copyright-protected work.

freely used as long as some basic conditions are met. Nevertheless, it is growing more common for textual material to also be offered under a Creative Commons license; the popular web pages on citing sources and avoiding plagiarism from the Duke University Libraries, for example, are made available under a CC license that permits users to copy, distribute, and modify those resources as long as appropriate credit is given to the source.[11]

Creative Commons licenses are used by creators and other copyright holders to alert potential users that the works are available for reuse under specified conditions (Creative Commons 2014b). Those conditions typically include a requirement of attribution (the "BY" provision), a stipulation about whether or not commercial uses are permitted without additional permission (the "NC," for noncommercial use only, provision) and, sometimes, a statement either forbidding derivative works or requiring that derivatives be offered under the same licensing terms (the "NoDerivs" or "ShareAlike" provisions). Once a copyright holder affixes a CC license, users can rely on this prior permission to reproduce and distribute the work as long as these conditions are met. Thus the Duke pages on citation and plagiarism can be used only for noncommercial purposes and with proper attribution, while derivative versions are permitted as long as they are shared under the same terms—the license is an "Attribution-NonCommercial-ShareAlike" license.

Creative Commons licenses can be very useful and time-saving when a teacher or researcher needs an image or a song, for example, but does not care that it is a specific image or song. Then she can search using the Creative Commons search tools found on the CC website for a work that will suit her needs. When a particular work—this specific photo or that singular performance of a specified musical work—is required, it can be more difficult, and often impossible, to find a CC-licensed version.

---

11. See Duke University 2014. The CC license is indicated by the small icon in the bar at the bottom of the page.

Research Example—CC Licenses

For his upcoming presentation at a conference on grass-roots social movements, Professor DeJarne wants a photo of the antigovernment protest movements that took place in Cairo's Tahrir Square in early 2011. Since he needs a picture of the massive crowds but not any specific photo, he uses the CC search function on Flickr and locates a photo that will suit his need. By clicking on the words "Some Rights Reserved" on the bottom of the page, he learns that he is free to share and remix the photo, subject only to the condition that he provides attribution to the copyright holder. For this particular photo, the owner is identified only as "yamaha gangsta," so Professor DeJarne includes that name, along with acknowledgement that the photo came from Flickr and the date on which it was downloaded, on the final slide of his presentation. The Creative Commons license has made this process very quick, and Professor DeJarne feels more secure about using this photo than he would a commercial image or one found on the Internet without any licensing terms.

IS THERE A SPECIFIC EXCEPTION IN THE COPYRIGHT LAW THAT ALLOWS MY PROPOSED USE?

When we speak of a "specific" exception to copyright's exclusive rights, we refer to all of the exceptions other than fair use. The copyright law devotes sixteen sections and nearly one third of its pages to exceptions— cases where an activity that would otherwise infringe the exclusive rights of the copyright holder are declared to be "not an infringement." The first exception listed (section 107) is fair use, which is a flexible and indeterminate balancing test that we shall discuss in detail shortly. All of the other exceptions (sections 108 through 122) are spelled out in much greater detail, both in terms of the exclusive rights they address and the requirements that must be met in order to come under the scope of the exception and thus avoid committing an infringement.

In creating a five-step process for determining how to use a copyright work, we intentionally ask about specific exceptions before turning to fair use. Because they are more detailed and circumscribed, the specific exceptions apply to narrower situations. But when they apply, they offer more certainty that the covered activity is not an infringement. Fair use, because of its flexible structure, is always more risk analysis than it is certainty. So it is wise to look at the specific exceptions first and rely on them when possible, turning to fair use only in those situations, and they are numerous for scholars, where a specific exception does not apply.

There are really only two specific exceptions that are designed for scholarly activity; both are specifically for teaching. Before we turn to those, however, it is worth noting that section 108 of the Copyright Act contains a set of exceptions for libraries and archives, which, although they are not directly used by scholars, are still important because of the support they provide to scholarship. Section 108 allows libraries and archives to make copies of both published and unpublished works for the purpose of preservation, to provide copies to researchers for the purpose of scholarship and research, and to participate in interlibrary loan arrangements. These activities are fundamental for supporting the process of scholarship, so it is worthwhile to note the existence of the exceptions and that they are somewhat controversial as more and more library activities are carried out digitally rather than in print.

Performances and Displays in Face-to-Face Teaching

Both of the specific exceptions for teaching involve public performance rights. The first of the two, and the easier by far to explain, involves performances presented in the course of face-to-face teaching, while the second deals with online transmissions of performances and displays. In the face-to-face context, most performances are permitted, even though they are public performances that would otherwise be under the exclusive control of the copyright holder.[12]

The exception for face-to-face teaching allows all forms of performance and display as long as they take place during teaching activities in a "classroom or similar place devoted to instruction" as part of the work of a nonprofit educational institution (17 U.S.C. § 110(1)). This language has become important as more and more for-profit educational institutions arise, since they are not eligible for this exception or, more importantly, the parallel exception for online teaching.

In addition to these requirements—that the instruction be face-to-face, sponsored by a nonprofit institution, and in a classroom or similar place—there is only one other rule about these permissible performances. Performances of audiovisual works must be given using a lawfully made copy of the work. Thus it is permissible to show a DVD of a Shakespeare play, for example, if the instructor has purchased the DVD, borrowed it from a library, or been loaned it by a neighbor. Only if the instructor knows or should know that the copy is a pirated copy—if it was bought on a street corner from an itinerant vendor, perhaps—is the performance not authorized. One issue that is not wholly clear is whether a performance of a DVD borrowed through a service like Netflix is similarly authorized. Nothing in the law itself would prevent such a performance, since the copies loaned by Netflix are certainly lawfully made; the issue is that Netflix's terms of use state that subscribers can use the DVDs for their personal use only (Netflix 2014). While a performance of a Netflix DVD in a live classroom would not be a copyright infringement, due to the face-to-face exception, it might involve the subscriber in a breach of contract because of these terms of use. No court, however, has considered

---

12. Public performances are defined in the Copyright Act as those given in "a place open to the public" or anywhere where "a substantial number of people outside of a normal circle of a family and its social acquaintances is gathered" (17 U.S.C. §101 under "publicly"). While the copyright holder has no control at all over private performances (those that are viewed only by a family and its social acquaintances), it is clear that a classroom performance is a public performance that would be infringing were it not for the face-to-face teaching exceptions.

this issue, and it might well be that a professor who rented a DVD from Netflix on her personal account and showed it to her class could still be considered to have made only a personal use.

It is important to understand the breadth of this exception. It allows not just the showing of a film or DVD, but also performances of music, live readings of literary works, and the display of images in face-to-face classrooms. These activities are so common that we tend to take them for granted, but, without this exception to the copyright law, all of them would either require individual permission or be impermissible.

Because the language of this exception is fairly broad and vague—teaching "activities" and a place "devoted to instruction"—its interpretation is rather open-ended. It clearly applies beyond the confines of a credit-bearing course to allow performances in other teaching settings. Librarians, for example, can rely on this exception in providing bibliographic instruction, and professional groups may fall within its ambit during training programs. Student groups present a situation where individual consideration is probably needed; a student group discussing a topic related to the curriculum or in some other way that is clearly educational may be able to use this exception, but student film societies that are organized purely for entertainment and diversion clearly cannot.

Transmissions of Performances and Displays

The 1976 Copyright Act has always contained a provision for using performances and displays as part of distance education, but the original form of that exception contemplated only closed-circuit television instruction, so it quickly became outmoded. In 2002, Congress amended this exception, section 110(2) of the act, to allow for transmissions of performances and displays through online teaching methods. The bill that made these amendments was called the Technology, Education and Copyright Harmonization Act, or TEACH Act for short, and this provision continues to be called by that name (Pub. L. No. 107-273, 116 Stat. 1758, 1910). The TEACH Act governs transmissions through online systems, including the course management systems that now are a part of so many academic classes, of performances like music, recorded readings, and films, as well as displays of slides. The TEACH Act has quite a few rules and restrictions, many designed to mirror the limitations that exist in the physical environment. The result is a provision with the potential to be very useful for online education but also with a fairly high bar for compliance.

The first thing we should note about the TEACH Act is that since it applies to performances and displays, it cannot be used to justify placing textual material in an online system. Texts per se are not the kind of material that is subject to performance or display, so placing scanned text in a course management system must be justified, if it can be, by fair use and not by reliance on TEACH. TEACH does help, however, when the material to be transmitted is a recording *reading* of a text, which is, of course, a performance.

The TEACH Act describes some limitations on the amounts of performances and displays that may be transmitted. It specifically allows the transmission of the entirety of recorded performances of nondramatic literary or musical works. This means that a whole symphony performance, the complete reading of a play or set of poems, or an entire CD of songs may be transmitted, subject to the other requirements of TEACH being met. All other performances, however, can be transmitted only in "reasonable and limited portions." So while an entire Mozart symphony may be transmitted, only a portion of his opera *Die Fledermaus* can be used in distance education because the latter is a dramatic musical work. Most significantly, TEACH does not authorize the transmission of an entire film. So while a face-to-face class can watch a whole movie together, the same film can be used in a distance education setting only in reasonable and limited portions.[13]

---

13. The legislative history of the TEACH Act does seem to suggest that an entire film might be a reasonable transmission in rare cases. But in practice, if an institution wants to stream entire films for course view over a course management system, it will likely turn to a fair use argument, as will be discussed below, rather than trying to shoehorn that transmission into the TEACH Act.

The text of the TEACH Act is equally unspecific about the amount of a display that may be transmitted, saying only that a transmission is limited to "an amount comparable to that which is typically displayed in the course of a live classroom session." So if a teacher would normally show twenty-five slides in her live art history class, those twenty-five slides can also be scanned and transmitted to students through an online system. If we follow the exact language of this sentence, it would seem that those twenty-five slides should be removed from the system when the slides for the next class are being uploaded. This result, while labor-intensive, is in keeping with the overall attempt in TEACH to mimic the limitations that exist in live classrooms.

In addition to its restrictions on the portions of materials that may be used for online education, the TEACH Act imposes a number of other requirements, some of which must be met by the instructor, some by the technology department, and some by the institution.[14]

The most general requirements imposed by TEACH on transmissions of copyrighted performances and displays are those at the institutional level. First, institutions eligible to take advantage of this provision are defined as government bodies or accredited nonprofit educational institutions. Note that in addition to paralleling the nonprofit limitation applied for face-to-face performances, in this instance Congress saw fit to add that the educational institutions must be accredited. These eligible institutions must also have policies in place that "accurately describe, and promote compliance with" copyright laws.[15] Finally, the institution must provide notice to its students that they may be using materials in their course that are subject to copyright protection.

---

14. A helpful way to work through these requirements is provided in the "TEACH Act toolkit" available on the website of North Carolina State University (NCSU 2011).

15. 17 U.S.C. § 110(2). This provision represents one of the places where the copyright law extends a benefit only to those institutions that enact a copyright policy; the other is found in §512, the so-called "safe harbor" that protects Internet service providers from liability for infringement committed by users without the actual knowledge of the ISP.

Requirements imposed on the instructor who wishes to rely on the TEACH Act are primarily related to the decisions about what content to use in a course. The performances or displays that are transmitted must be "made at the direction of, or under the actual supervision of an instructor as an integral part of a class session offered as a regular part of systematic mediated instructional activities." This means that TEACH does not authorize transmissions made in connection with those informal or ad hoc groups that often work on university and college campuses. The provision goes on to say that the performance or display must be "directly related and of material assistance to the teaching content of the transmission" (17 U.S.C. §110(2)). Here the point seems to be to rule out transmitted performances that are intended as mere entertainments or rewards, rather than necessary content. And of course, the instructor will ultimately be responsible for deciding on the portions of the copyrighted performances and displays that will be transmitted, in accordance with the limitations described above. The best rule of thumb for deciding what is a "reasonable and limited portion," after all, is the pedagogical necessity that is driving the transmission in the first place. If no more is used than is justified by the teaching purpose, the chances are very good that this qualification will be met.[16]

It is with its technological requirements that the TEACH Act becomes most problematic for implementation in college and university courses. The first requirement, that receipt of the transmission by limited "to the extent technologically feasible" only to officially enrolled students, is not really very difficult, since most campus course management systems (Blackboard, Moodle, etc.) permit this sort of closed access; indeed, it is usually the system default setting. But it is worth remembering that setting the course page for "guest" access will undermine TEACH Act compliance. Additionally, some of the commercial systems that are increasingly used for course content delivery, like Google Docs, Word-

---

16. We use the language of probability deliberately here, since as of this writing no court cases have interpreted the TEACH Act or provided guidance about the meaning of its terms.

Press, or even YouTube, are not TEACH Act–compliant in their normal configuration, and steps must be taken to secure access before TEACH-authorized transmissions can be made.

Another technological requirement in the TEACH Act is that the transmission must not interfere with technological protection measures used by copyright owners to limit or control access and copying. These electronic protection measures (EPMs), or digital rights management (DRM) systems, as they are also known, will be discussed in more detail later in this section and in chapter 6, but here we must note that by the terms of the TEACH Act and under other provisions of the law it is not permissible to "circumvent" these technological access controls even in cases where the underlying use (the transmission of a performance or display) would itself be authorized by TEACH. So, for example, it seems not to be permissible to upload a digital file from a DVD for transmission under TEACH if the DVD is encoded with some form of protection system, the most common of which is CSS, or Content Scrambling System. The TEACH Act anticipated this issue, and we will have more to say about it shortly.

The last requirement in this long list of TEACH Act hurdles is that the transmitting body must "apply technological measures that reasonably prevent" retention of the transmitted work by students beyond the duration of the class session or further distribution of the material by them to others. These technological measures are different from those referred to above, which are employed by the copyright holder; the latter we must simply leave alone, while we must be proactive in regard to the former. What exactly are measures that "reasonably" prevent retention and redistribution is not particularly clear. The legislative history of the act uses streaming of films and music as an example, so we know the measures do not have to be perfect. Indeed, for many performances that are transmitted, streaming those transmissions (so they cannot be easily downloaded) will be the easiest way to comply with this part of TEACH. Again, it is worth noting that some commercial platforms for delivery of content, such as iTunes U, from which material is nearly always down-loadable, are not likely to be usable under TEACH.

The choice of technological measures to use for images is not as clear-cut. It may be sufficient to save the files in a format (like PDF) where it is possible to disable the "right-click" ability to copy or download the image. One university developed its own technological solution for this part of TEACH Act compliance, with software that imposes an empty and transparent file over the original image so that when an attempt is made to save the image only the empty file is captured.[17]

In order to transmit any of these performances or displays, copies must obviously be made to be uploaded into the delivery system, usu-ally a course management platform. The law specifically allows for these "ephemeral" copies for TEACH Act purposes (17 U.S.C. § 112(b)). If a digital file of the performance or display is available without technologi-cal protections, it can simply be copied into the platform, with all other requirements met, for transmission. But as we have already noted, the law does not allow for circumvention of technological locks. When a digital copy of a work is either unavailable or is protected with digital coding that is designed to prevent copying, like CSS on a DVD, the law as amended by TEACH permits making a digital file from an analogy copy. Thus it is often the case that in order to transmit a portion of a film, the digital file must be created from an analog copy (e.g., VHS) of the film. This is true even if the institution owns a DVD of the film, if that DVD is encoded with the Content Scrambling System or some similar electronic "lock."

Teaching Example—Hybrid Courses

Professor Hudson teaches a course in sociology in which she routinely shows two movies and has students read several articles from the online journal databases at her

---

17. This software, developed at North Carolina State University and called "WolfLocker" had been available to other institutions for open source download but, as of this writing, cannot be found on the NCSU website.

university's library. She would now like to save some class time by making the films available through the university's course management system (CMS) so that students can view them outside of class. Since she is creating a course site in the CMS, she also wonders about providing copies of the journal articles there so that students have "one-stop" access to all the course materials. In regard to the two films, she must decide if she can reduce the amount of film that the students watch to a "reasonable and limited portion" in order for the transmission through the CMS page to be permissible under TEACH. If it is absolutely necessary for the students to watch the whole film, it is safest to continue to show it in a face-to-face setting (although a fair use justification might be possible, as we shall see). She must also make sure that uploading the films does not involve circumventing electronic protection measures and that the other requirements of the TEACH Act are met. Her best option for the articles is to provide links in her CMS page that take the students directly to the specific articles within the licensed database. If she decides she must make copies, this must be justified not under the TEACH Act, which does not cover copies of text, but by fair use.

IS MY PROPOSED USE A "FAIR USE"?

Fair use is the single most important exception in copyright law for scholarship and education. Scholars depend on its broad and flexible scope nearly every day of their professional lives. Even incorporating a quotation from another author into an essay or article is dependent on fair use; it is simply a well-established and uncontroversial example of the fair use analysis.

It is important to realize how indispensable fair use is in order to counter the widespread notion that fair use is too indeterminate to be reliable for educators and scholars. There is a great deal of misinformation floating around about fair use, some of it from those who want to make their opinions seem like fact, but much from people who are simply misinformed or only partially informed. Fair use is intentionally open-ended—some would say vague—because that indeterminacy ensures that fair use, alone among the copyright exceptions, can be adapted to new technologies and permit uses that were not even imaginable when the copyright statute was written. There is a common joke that only nine people—the justices of the Supreme Court—really know whether or not a particular use is fair because only they have a genuinely final say. This is true, in its way, but it fails to recognize that many fair uses take place all the time without generating lawsuits or even being very controversial. The fact that fair use is flexible does not mean that it is unreliable; there is a great deal of space for uncontroversial fair use, even though there are some vigorous disagreements about the edges of the doctrine. Within that uncontroversial space are many scholarly activities, and we will try to pay attention to both those safe practices and the controversial ones.

Because fair use does have this element of risk analysis, it properly comes fourth in our five-question procedure. If a work that one wants to use does not have a copyright at all, of course, there is no reason to turn to fair use. If, on the other hand, a proposed use of a copyrighted work is governed by a license or a specific exception in the law, good risk management suggests relying on those rather than on fair use. But many, many scholarly uses are not decided by these first three questions, and for those, fair use is an intentionally flexible and open-ended option. In some cases the proposed use simply was not considered by lawmakers when the current law was written in the 1960s and 70s. In other cases, all of the requirements for the exception cannot be met for some reason. For these situations, the fair use analysis should not be neglected.

The fair use analysis—the determination of whether or not a particular use is a fair or not—is based on four factors the statute tells us to consider (17 U.S.C. § 107). This list of factors is explicitly not exclusive; the fair use determination is really a decision about what is equitable in the specific circumstances, and the factors are simply a guide for considering those circumstances. Because fair use is so fact-specific, it is inevitably necessary, as we consider each factor, to look at court cases to see how it has been applied to specific fact patterns in the past. Often these cases provide avenues for thinking about the specifics of a new and undetermined use that is being proposed. But the fact that we look at court cases should not lead to the conclusion that every fair use, or even most, leads to lawsuits or require judges to make a determination.

The Factor Analysis

The first fair use factor is "the purpose and character of the [proposed] use." In recent years this factor, always considered important, has come to dominate the fair use analysis because of the emphasis placed on transformative uses, about which we will say more shortly. For scholars, however, the qualification added by the text of the copyright law to its statement of the first factor is very significant—"including whether such use is of a commercial nature or is for nonprofit educational purposes." This qualification seems to set up a continuum, with scholarly uses on the positive side of the balance, favored in the fair use analysis, and commercial uses on the negative side. Nevertheless, it is not true that all educational uses are automatically considered fair use, nor is it impossible for a commercial use to be considered fair. To prove the first part of this point we need only look at the "course pack" cases, where reproduction of published materials by commercial copy shops for inclusion in packets of course readings that were sold to students was twice held to not qualify as fair use (Basic Books v. Kinko's Graphics Corp., 758 F.Supp. 1522 (S.D.N.Y. 1991); Princeton University Press v. Michigan Document Service, 99 F. 3d 1381 (6th cir. 1996)). It is significant that both these cases involved a commercial intermediary; while no court has determined whether or not a course pack created entirely within an educational institution with no profit motive at all would be fair use, these cases do show that not everything done in the service of teaching will be considered fair.

As for commercial uses, most of the cases that reach the federal court do involve uses that have a profit motive, for the simple reason that these situations motivate the rights holder to sue with the hope of recovering damages. In the classic case involving a transformative use, *Campbell v. Acuff Rose Music*, for example, fair use was found by the United States Supreme Court even though the reuse of the song "Oh, Pretty Woman" by the rap group 2 Live Crew was unabashedly commercial (510 U.S. 569 (1994)). The heart of the analysis in this case was that the parody created by 2 Live Crew of Roy Orbison's classic song was transformative because it created a new work that had a social function and value independent of the original and was not a market substitution that might threaten sales of the original; no one would buy one as an adequate substitute for the other.

Since the 2 Live Crew case, courts have mostly looked for a transformative purpose when analyzing the first fair use factor, and that analysis can help us discriminate more finely among academic uses. Some educational uses, such as putting a scan of a book chapter into a learning management system so that all students in a class can read it, do not have an obvious transformative effect. The clear purpose of this use is to prevent students from having to purchase a book when only a chapter or so will be needed. This use may still be fair use, especially if the portion used is small, but it is much less clear that it is transformative.[18] On the other hand, using some film stills in an academic book where the content of the images is subjected to scholarly analysis is more clearly transformative, as are compilations of film clips or printed excerpts if there is additional scholarly content provided that repurposes the works to make a new and different argument that was not anticipated in the original. A recent court case, for example, turned on whether it was fair use to reprint, without

---

18. In the ongoing case against Georgia State University over e-reserves, the trial court judge held that the scanning of excerpts for electronic access as course content was not transformative. Nevertheless, she still found that most of the excerpts were fair use, indicating that transformativeness is not an absolute prerequisite for fair use. This is one of several aspects of the District Court ruling that the plaintiff publishers are appealing.

permission, letters written by an early twentieth-century figure in the context of a biography. Because this scholarly activity pretty clearly transforms the original purpose of the letters, the court supported fair use.[19]

The Second and Third Fair Use Factors

The second factor considered in a fair use analysis does not get the kind of attention that it should. When courts consider "the nature of the copyrighted work" that is being used, they basically look at only two features: whether it is published or unpublished and where it falls on a continuum from purely factual works to highly creative ones. It is easier to make a fair use of a work that is published and more factual; more difficult if the work is highly creative and/or unpublished. Several commentators have suggested that this factor could provide a much richer opportunity for the courts to understand the particular market and incentives for creation behind a copyrighted work (see, e.g., Kasunic 2008); academic works, for example, are created for different reasons and with different economic motives than a novel or a new popular song. Unfortunately, courts have not pursued this opportunity, and the analysis of the second fair use factor is usually truncated and seldom decisive of the question.

The third factor in the fair use analysis is the "amount and substantiality" of the portion that is used. Here the simple rule of thumb, when making a fair use argument, is that less is always better than more. For educational and scholarly uses, we can add that one should use no more than is necessary to make the scholarly or pedagogical point that drives the use in the first place. This approach is sometimes referred to as "the Goldilocks rule"; one should use an amount that is "just right," neither too much nor too little, to accomplish the educational purpose. This factor, of

---

19. The case pitted academic author Carol Shloss against the estate of James Joyce and involved the letters of Joyce's daughter Lucia. Although the case settled before it went to trial, the payment by the Joyce estate of almost a quarter of a million dollars in legal fees incurred by Dr. Shloss indicates the strength of the fair use claim. A description of the case can be found in CIS 2014.

course, is something that is easily in the control of the user, so if doubts arise about whether or not a particular use is fair, one can always opt to reduce the portion used and run through the fair use analysis again for the smaller portion. This will not always transform an unfair use into a fair one, but in certain contexts (in a learning management or e-reserves system, for example) it can help a great deal.

The issue of the "substantiality" of the portion used is rather diffuse. Legislative history suggests that the word was used to indicate that it should be harder to make a fair use of a portion that is deemed "the heart" of a work. In a well-known case involving the memoirs of former President Gerald Ford, the Supreme Court rejected a fair use defense on the part of a magazine that had published a small excerpt without permission in part because the court thought it was the heart of the work—it was the couple of paragraphs in which Ford directly addressed his reasons for pardoning Richard Nixon (Harper & Row Publishers v. Nation Enterprises, 471 U.S. 539 (1985)). But this reasoning is quite rare, and determining what is the heart of a work is very subjective. For academic uses it is often the case that the work is being used to make some point or argument quite different from the original, so often what is the heart of the original will not be at issue in these fair use situations. In one context, that of readings in an e-reserve or learning management system, some institutions believe that, in order to avoid using the heart of a work, only supplemental readings, rather than required texts, should be made available as digital reproductions.

Fourth Factor: Effect on the Potential Markets for the Original

In the 1985 case involving Gerald Ford's memoirs, the Supreme Court opined that this fourth fair use factor—effect of the use on the potential market for or value of the original—was the most important fair use consideration. Since that time, however, the first factor has gained importance because of the emphasis on transformativeness described above.

One of the criteria for transformation in the fair use analysis is that the new use does not compete with the original in the same market. Thus the first factor has, with this analysis, had a substantial impact on the fourth factor as well and has somewhat eclipsed it in importance. Nevertheless, this fourth factor retains substantial importance, especially in those cases where the proposed use is not obviously a transformation so that the impact on the market must be evaluated separately from the first factor. The central question to ask in this situation is "Is the proposed use simply a substitute for purchasing the original?" If the answer to this question is yes, this factor will probably count against a fair use determination.

When we look at this fourth fair use factor, it is very clear that the factors interrelate. The analysis of transformativeness is one such inter-relation, between the first and fourth factors. Another is the relationship between the third factor (amount) and this fourth factor. If a small enough portion of an original work is used, it is much more difficult to argue that the use was a substitute for a purchase and therefore had an adverse effect on the market for the original. This is why some schools require that teaching faculty certify, when asking for a book excerpt to be placed on electronic reserve, that the instructor would not require purchase of the book if reserve options were not available; for a single chapter from a longer book that is assigned as supplemental reading, this is a plausible assurance, but it is less believable when it is clear that large portions of scanned works are being used to provide the entire reading list for a class. Between these two extremes, electronic reserves are highly controversial, as evidenced by the lawsuit going on over them at the time of this writing, brought by Oxford University Press, Cambridge University Press and Sage Publications against Georgia State University.[20]

---

20. The case is called Cambridge University Press v. Patton et al. and was filed in the Northern District Court of Georgia, in Atlanta, on April 15, 2008. The trial court decision, issued on May 11, 2012, was largely a victory for Georgia State and its faculty, since infringement was found in only five of the seventy-five challenged readings. The publishers that brought the lawsuit have appealed that decision to the 11th Circuit Court of Appeals, and the issue is pending as of this writing.

Complicating the question of market harm is the growing availability of licensing options for academic writings as well as music and film. Even when small portions of a work are used, some rights holders will maintain that there is market harm when the market for a license is considered. The Internet has allowed these licensing transactions to become much more convenient and efficient. Carried to an extreme, this development could be taken to mean that fair use of a particular type of content would vanish once the licensing markets were sufficiently established, but this is clearly not what was intended when Congress adapted the judicial fair use doctrine into the law. Thus the question becomes which licensing markets should, or should not, count when we consider market harm? The analysis of transformativeness is one response to this question, suggesting that some reuses are not anticipated or even likely to be approved of by rights holders in the original; those are cases where fair use retains its core function. In the Georgia State e-reserves case, the trial judge held that the relevant market was that for digital excerpts, and when publishers did not make such specific licenses available, the fourth factor did not weigh against fair use. In other cases, the argument is about whether reliance on a licensing market to suggest that fair use is either irrelevant or even more severely limited constitutes circular reasoning—using the availability of permission as a factor in deciding if permission is needed in the first place. This is not the place to rehearse the details of this argument, but it is important to know, when making a fair use determination, what licensing opportunities are available and whether the proposed use is the kind of thing that rights holders customarily would license.

Controversial and Uncontroversial Fair Use

We have already discussed electronic reserves in some detail as we have proceeded through a description of the fair use factor analysis. Before turning to concluding remarks about fair use, it may be helpful to look at some other common academic uses and consider the degree to which they are controversial.

Uncontroversial Fair Use Examples

The most obvious and ubiquitous example of fair use for scholarship and teaching is the quotation. The use of a small passage from another person's work in one's own is the foundation of a great deal of scholarship, since all scholars, as Isaac Newton is reported to have said, stand on the shoulders of giants. Fair use supports this practice, since the labor and uncertainty of getting permission for each quotation, were it needed, would make so much scholarship impossible. Also, this example allows us to see how fair use also underlies the free speech guarantee in the US Constitution; if permission were needed for every quotation, rights holders would be able to use copyright to prevent criticism and disagreement. Fair use prevents copyright from becoming such an engine of censorship.

The fair use right to quotation extends beyond words quoted from a text document. Reuse of graphs, images, film stills and other copyright-protected materials, in small portions and where those materials are subjected to scholarly criticism and comment, is also an uncontroversial example of fair use.

In an age where the use of film in teaching is increasingly common, teachers often need to assemble compilations of film clips in order to compare techniques or treatments of a theme, or simply to make a particular teaching point. Since compiling such clip compilations requires reproduction, not merely performance, reliance on fair use is necessary to support this practice. Here again, this is a fairly noncontroversial application of fair use for teaching.

From the example of film clips we can extrapolate and suggest that many kinds of incorporation of copyrighted works into a new work of scholarship—what we might call "remix scholarship"—will also be a fair use that does not generate dispute. A class project to use materials from popular culture to create public service videos on environmental or social issues might be an example of such remix scholarship that fair use supports.

Fair Use Controversies

Fair use for course packs—custom printed collections of readings for a particular class created by excerpting from published works—is an issue on which courts have ruled a couple of times, as mentioned above. Since both cases ruled against these compilations being fair use, it is tempting to remove this from the category of controversies and suggest that the matter is closed. But both cases decided on the issue of course packs involved commercial copy shops that made the collections at the direction of professors and sold them to students. The commercial nature of these intermediaries was very important in both decisions, and no case has ruled on the fair use analysis for a course pack created in-house at a nonprofit educational institution.

The example of electronic reserves has made the undecided aspect of course packs of central importance, since electronic reserves are, essentially, in-house course packs in digital form. In the court case against Georgia State University over electronic reserves, the plaintiff argues that this analogy settles the matter against a finding of fair use. But the university maintained, and the trial court agreed, that the situation is different in an essential way—the first factor of the fair use analysis favors the university in a way it did not favor Kinko's or Michigan Document Service. Nevertheless, this remains a very live controversy, with many institutions implementing policies about what they will or will not do regarding e-reserves in order to preserve the best argument for fair use that they can. In all likelihood, this "risk analysis" approach to fair use will continue to be needed as digital course readings remain controversial.

Another lawsuit that was filed against UCLA, and dismissed on procedural grounds, brought attention to a different fair use controversy, streaming of digital videos through a closed learning management system so that they can be viewed outside of class and on a student's own schedule. Although this practice has similarities to the in-class performances allowed under section 110, it is not exactly the same. Nor is it obviously allowed by the TEACH Act provisions. Thus fair use is at the heart of this controversy, with the plaintiff arguing that licenses must be obtained for every video streamed, even when a physical copy of the DVD is already owned. UCLA and a few other institutions defend this practice as fair use that causes no market harm not also caused by the well-established face-to-face performance exception. In dismissing this lawsuit, the trial court judge called the fair use justification for this practice "plausible," but did not actually make any ruling about it. So here, as with e-reserves, institutions will need to make careful judgments balancing pedagogical needs with institutional risk tolerance.

Fair Use Decisions in Academia

As the above examples should make clear, fair use is something that is used in academia every single day, yet it is also the source of great controversy and even, sometimes, litigation. Because we cannot know with absolute certainty that a particular reuse of copyright material is or is not a fair use, short of a lawsuit, a form of risk analysis must always be part of our thinking about copyright in scholarship. Academic institutions have a natural aversion to risk, of course, but that sensible attitude should not be allowed to have a "chilling effect" on activities that are necessary for scholarship or that significantly advance teaching. Since we have no choice but to rely on fair use in some ways (and that is a good thing!), we need to take a reasoned approach as individual scholars and have balanced policies as institutions. Some fair uses are so uncontroversial as to require little concern at all. Others may need an institutional policy that sets boundaries, encourages good faith consideration of fair use, and offers educational support and alternative techniques to faculty members. For example, if a faculty member determines that scanning a particular course reading to be placed in a learning management system page would exceed fair use, she can be directed to options for linking to a licensed digital copy, to physical reserves, or to guidance about how to reduce the scope of the reading so that it conforms with the institution's evaluation of fair use.

As part of this risk analysis, it is helpful to realize that copyright law provides some added security for academics. In the section of the law on remedies, where the financial and other penalties for copyright infringement are set out, there is a provision that substantially reduces the risk for employees of a nonprofit educational institution if they make an ultimately erroneous estimation of fair use (17 U.S.C. § 504(c)(2)). The provision says that such academics, if their fair use analysis is made in good faith, will not be at risk for the largest chunk of potential financial penalty, which is called "statutory" damages.[21] This provision is not a free pass, since other financial risks—actual damages and attorney's fees—are still in play, but it is a clear indication that Congress wished to avoid letting the uncertain nature of fair use prevent its exercise in the most socially valuable arena to which it applies.

One way that has been used frequently to manage the risk inherent in fair use decisions is to draft guidelines or best practices that are more specific than the fair use factors; it is important to understand the status of these efforts and the difference between them.

---

21. Good faith requires both subjective honesty and an objectively reasonable analysis.

Guidelines are usually negotiated statements of minimum standards that are agreed to by both user communities and rights holders. There have been very influential guidelines negotiated on multiple copies made for classroom distribution and for interlibrary loan programs.[22] Other guidelines that have been worked on for higher education have either failed to get consent of all parties or have had much less influence than these two. It is important to realize that none of these guidelines actually have the force of law; there is simply no legal standard for fair use that says, for example, that you can reproduce only 10 percent of a written work, or 30 seconds of a piece of music.[23] The guidelines are recommendations, and they almost always represent a minimum judgment about what might be permitted. They represent, in short, "safe harbors" rather than the full extent of fair use for a given situation. Often an institution that is drafting policy about fair use will look at guidelines and even incorporate portions of them into the policy, which can be a sensible course for the risk-averse. But guidelines are situation-specific and often date very quickly as technology changes; excessive reliance on guidelines undermines the very virtues of the flexible fair use provision.

Best practices represent a different approach, in which practitioners in a certain area define for themselves what they believe are good approaches to fair use for the particular situations that arise frequently in that area. The Center for Media and Social Impact (formerly the Center for Social Media) at American University, for example, has been very active in drafting best practices of media literacy and for documentary film making.[24] Careful research and analysis goes into these statements, but they are not negotiated with rights holders. Thus they may offer

22. A copy of the guidelines on multiple copies for classroom use is available at http://libraries.uky.edu/page.php?lweb_id=295. The guidelines on interlibrary loan can be found at www.unc.edu/~unclng/ILL-guidelines.htm.

23. In the Georgia State lawsuit over e-reserves, the trial judge rejected the application of these guidelines in toto, but did apply a rigid 10 percent or one chapter (whichever is less) standard as the acceptable amount for fair use in that circumstance.

24. The full set of best practice codes from the CMSI is found at www.cmsimpact.org/fair-use/best-practices.

somewhat less security from lawsuits than guidelines are intended to. The key to best practices, however, is to offer a statement about what current "industry practice" is in a particular endeavor. Their role in court, should a conflict arise, would be precisely to offer a baseline of the customary behavior that practitioners feel is necessary against which to measure a challenged activity. Although no cases involving best practices have reached the courts to my knowledge, the statement of best practices for documentary filmmakers has had an important impact on the ability of filmmakers to get insurance against infringement claims, since the major insurers now accept adherence to it as evidence of copyright compliance (see Aufderheide 2007).

In January 2012, the Association of Research Libraries released a *Code of Best Practices in Fair Use for Academic and Research Libraries* (ARL 2012). Although focused, obviously, on library activities, some of these best practices are relevant for teaching and research. For example, one of the "principles" discussed involves electronic reserves. The principle essentially asserts that this practice can be fair use, and the code then lists some "limitations" that are considered important for defending a fair use claim. It also lists "enhancements," which are ways to strengthen a fair use defense, although they are not considered necessary. This code of best practices can assist scholars as well as librarians in thinking through the circumstances that can make fair use more or less applicable to a particular practice.

Finally, we cannot leave a discussion of fair use without noting the impact of the so-called "anti-circumvention" rules on fair use in academia. We will discuss these issues in more depth in chapter 6, but a brief summary is needed here. As part of the Digital Millennium Copyright Act of 1998, a provision was added to the copyright law that made it illegal to "circumvent a technical protection measure that effectively controls access to a work protected" by copyright (17 U.S.C. § 1201(a)). These rules have generally been taken to prevent "ripping" and other kinds of circumvention of technological protection measures even in cases where the use that was intended and for which the copy was being made would be authorized by fair use or some other exception. With the TEACH Act provision (section110(2)), we see that Congress specifically wrote rules to allow authorized transmissions without permitting circumvention, so this conclusion has some support; most of the time "digital locks" should not be circumvented even for a legal purpose.

Nevertheless, Congress imagined that this anti-circumvention law might have undesirable consequences, and it decided to authorize the Library of Congress to declare exemptions to the rules for certain classes of works every three years. In October 2012, the Library of Congress included in those exemptions a relatively broad rule that allows academics to circumvent digital locks for scholarly purposes (37 C.F.R. Part 201). This exemption does not change the definition of fair use, but it does specify a small group of educational purposes, within the broader category of fair use, for which circumvention is permitted. The exemption applies only to lawfully made and acquired DVDs that are protected by Content Scrambling System (CSS). It does not require that the DVD be part of a university's library collection (as an earlier rule did); the DVD can come from anywhere as long as it is not pirated or stolen. But it applies only to DVDs that use CSS; it does not, for example, apply to Blu-Ray discs or to video games. For such DVDs protected with CSS, *college and university faculty, and college and university students of film and media studies (but not other students), are permitted to circumvent* in order to *incorporate short portions of motion pictures into new works for the purpose of criticism, comment, and education.*

This exemption opens a window for educational uses that require circumvention, and it is now broader than at any time since the law was passed a decade ago. Faculty members are now permitted to circumvent DRM systems when doing so is necessary, for example, to compile a set of film clips to be used in teaching. Also, those types of "remix scholarship" discussed above are also now likely to be purposes, pretty clearly fair uses, for which technological locks need no longer be an obstacle. The rule specifies that circumvention is allowed only when short film clips are being incorporated into *new* works, such as a remix, an educational video, or a clip compilation. Thus it prevents technological protection measures from becoming a disabling obstacle for precisely those kinds of transformative educational uses that are, in themselves, most likely to be fair use.

WHO SHOULD I ASK FOR PERMISSION?

If these first four questions—about the public domain, licensing, specific copyright exceptions, and fair use—have failed to offer a justification for the particular use of copyrighted material under consideration, the option of asking for permission from the rights holder always remains.[25] Copyright infringement is always cured by permission; if the rights holder authorizes the use that you have in mind, you can proceed with confidence, at least as far as copyright is concerned. When deciding to ask for permission, two considerations are extremely important.

First, it is necessary to be sure that the permission request accurately describes the proposed use, since the protection from an infringement claim extends only to what the copyright holder actually gave permission for. Permission to use copyrighted material in a book, for example, probably does not extend as far as digitizing that book and putting it out on the public Web. Likewise, permission to use material in a face-to-face classroom (which is unlikely to be necessary, given the scope of the 110(1) exception discussed above) would be unlikely to cover use of the same material in an online class. Thus it is important to describe the use accurately and as broadly as one can imagine will be necessary. If unanticipated new opportunities to use the resulting product arise, it is well to return to the rights holder to avoid misunderstanding.

The second major consideration, and the most common obstacle to getting permission, is deciding who to ask and getting a response from

25. One of the best books discussing how permission works and the difficulties that can arise in asking for permission from a copyright holder is Bielstein 2006.

that person or organization. First one must determine who the rights holder is. For books this is relatively easy, since most contain a copyright statement on the back, or "verso," of the title page or, for older works, at the back. Even here, however, publisher mergers and acquisitions can make it difficult to trace rights holders.[26] Blanket licenses on a campus, discussed above, may reduce the need to research specific rights holders in some cases, such as when musical performances are being planned. For films, several organizations offer both blanket performance licenses for campuses and a mechanism for individual permission requests; the Motion Picture Licensing Corporation (www.mplc.org/index/worldwide) and Swank Motion Pictures (www.swank.com) are two such collective rights organizations.

For academics who want to use textual works in ways or amounts that exceed fair use, one of the most useful organizations is the Copyright Clearance Center, which, like the motion picture agencies, provides a blanket license for campuses that covers course packs, e-reserves, and learning management system uses, among others, as well as individualized permissions. Many academic publishers have licensing contracts with the CCC, so even when permission is not instantaneously available, as it often is, the CCC can, in many cases, pursue the request on behalf of the potential user. Another place to look for permission when wishing to use the work of writers or visual artists is a Web database called the WATCH File, for "Writers, Artists and Their Copyright Holders" (University of Texas 2014b). This is a valuable resource for determining the literary or artistic representatives of writers, painters, and other artists; it often leads one to a law firm or literary agency that can grant reuse rights.

These organizations and databases can be very useful when looking for permission to use more traditionally published works. The difficulties arise, however, when no rights holder is easily identifiable or a putative rights holder simply does not respond to a permission request. One genre

---

26. The Web database called "FOB: Firms Out of Business" (University of Texas 2014a) provides some assistance for this problem.

for which it can be especially hard to find a rights holder is photography, since there is no easy and commonly employed way to identify who took a particular photograph or otherwise owns the rights. The Web presents similar difficulties since it is often unclear who owns the rights in a website, and the interconnectedness of the Web means that it is remarkably easy to move without a clear awareness from work owned by one person, who perhaps can be identified, to work owned by someone else, who may not be readily known. Finally, both individuals and corporations that own the rights in some content may not know how to respond to a permission request or may ignore one because intellectual property rights are not the core of their particular business. In these cases, the best that we can do is to make good faith efforts and recognize that if, after two or three unsuccessful attempts to get permission there is still no clear rights holder identified or no answer to an inquiry, the argument for fair use becomes much stronger. In these instances, the failure of good faith efforts to get permission can become a strong element in the fair use analysis because that failure indicates that there is no licensing market that will be harmed by the proposed use.

Once a rights holder is located and permission negotiated, scholarly users are often confused about what form the permission must take. Exclusive grants of permission—those that exclude anyone else from making a similar use of the copyrighted material—must be in writing. While non-exclusive permissions, which are by far the most common for scholars to obtain, do not have to be written, it would be foolish to rely on a purely oral OK. Instead, the best course is to get an e-mail or other document, no matter how informal, that shows the scope of the request and the required permission from the rights holder. Such e-mail should either be kept in an electronic file that is backed up and easy to relocate or be printed and retained.

Research Example—Permission

Dr. Stephens is completing a book on human anatomy, and he wants to use a work of art by Picasso—one of his famous abstract figures—as the frontispiece for the publication. The particular painting is not yet in the public domain and is subject to no license or specific copyright exception. Because the frontispiece will be entirely decorative and not integral to the argument of his book, Dr. Stephens does not believe its use would be fair use. Therefore, Dr. Stephens seeks and receives permission from the Picasso estate, for a fee that he considers reasonable. After the book has been published and gone out of print several years later, the copyright reverts to Dr. Stephens, and he decides to mount the book in an online, open access repository of scholarship maintained by his university. Even though Dr. Stephens owns the copyright in the book as a whole and is free to do this, he needs to ask the Picasso estate before including the frontispiece because the original permission he obtained did not include distribution on the Web. If such permission is not forthcoming or is too expensive, Dr. Stephens should exclude the frontispiece from the online copy of his book.

CONCLUSION

These five questions are each complex and require some effort to navigate. Nevertheless, if they are considered in order and the circumstances of any proposed use of copyrighted material examined through the lens they create, scholars and academics can proceed with much greater confidence as they create new research and teaching products built from the works that have gone before.

Copyright Management and the Dissemination of Scholarship

WHEN GALILEO discovered the moons of Saturn in 1610, he promptly wrote to fellow scientist Johannes Kepler about his discovery. But he sent the letter in a cipher so that no one, including Kepler, could read about his discovery before he wanted them to. Galileo's principal concern was not widespread dissemination of the knowledge he had gained, but rather having a mechanism to prove the priority of his observations (Wooten 2010, 120–22). Only after some time had elapsed did Galileo allow Kepler to publish the discovery. Biographer David Wooten (2010, 123) notes that Galileo was using Kepler rather as if he (Kepler) was running a scientific journal, and in the process, Galileo was stepping away from the then-dominant method of sharing scientific discoveries through limited circulation monographs. He did so, apparently, in order to be able to verify the priority of his discovery—what we would call "registration" in a discussion of the stages of publication—without revealing what he had found prematurely.

It is perhaps difficult for us to realize today that scholarly journals were not always a part of the process of disseminating knowledge and that the transition to such publication was not easy. One of the oldest such journals continuously in publication, *The Philosophical Transactions of the Royal Society*, originally published correspondence between various scientists and Henry Oldenberg, its first editor. The early history of that journal, which was founded in 1665, was marked by difficulties in persuading scientists to adopt this new, more public method of disseminating their work. Scientists such as Christian Huygens, an early contributor, were simply not inclined to publish their discoveries, and Oldenberg had to carefully cajole Huygens and many others into doing so (Hall 2002, 136–38). As we are again in a period of dramatic change regarding the dissemination of scholarship, it is well to remember this evolution and to recognize that what seems obvious today was not obvious in Oldenberg's time, just as the best forms of publication that will evolve in the coming years are not obvious to us.

The mode of dissemination that ultimately came to dominate scientific and scholarly communications, the learned journal, developed slowly and met some resistance. But it ultimately has served scholarship very well for over three and a half centuries. The advent of digital communication has, arguably, begun another process of radical transition in scholarly communications, and scholars today need to be aware of the ways in which that transition is occurring, patient with the various formats and business models that are evolving, and vigilant about protecting and considering all of the options available to them.

TRADITIONAL SCHOLARLY PUBLISHING AND ITS DISCONTENTS

The traditional system of scholarly publication had its origins—at least in England, with the Worshipful Company of Stationers and Newspaper Makers—virtually simultaneously with the growth of the medieval universities. As scholarship moved from the monasteries to more widely accessible venues, the importance of making written materials available to a larger group of readers led to a symbiotic relationship between the universities and the Stationers' Company (Talbot 1958). Although both universities and publishers changed a great deal over the subsequent centuries—including through the transition from a book-dominated model to one reliant on periodical publications—the relationship remained mutually beneficial.

In discussing this relationship in his *Books in the Digital Age*, Professor John B. Thompson (2205, 11) writes, "The two worlds of higher education, that of teaching and that of research, are dependent in many ways on the output of academic and higher education publishers, and yet those whose lives are spent within higher education know surprisingly little about this industry upon which their own activities—and to some extent their careers and livelihoods—depend." Yet digital technology, with the ability it provides for every person to become their own publisher if they choose, suggests that the dependence between scholars and publishers is lessening over time and that new models of disseminating scholarship will continue to evolve. A deeper understanding of the options for dissemination is simply a necessity for scholars today. It is important to examine exactly what has made the relationship between publishers and scholars so beneficial over so many years and to consider the degree to which the benefits gained in that traditional relationship can be replicated in the online environment or, perhaps, are simply no longer necessary.

Publishers have traditionally provided at least four types of services in the academic publication process: they have selected material deemed valuable, managed the process of evaluating and editing that material, provided production services (until recently, printing), and overseen distribution and marketing.[1] Having one's work published is also a way for authors to "register" their work in order to establish their claim to

---

1. These functions are enumerated and discussed in the preface to the report *University Publishing in a Digital Age* (Guthrie 2007, para. 4). For alternative lists of the functions of scholarly publishers, see Rowland 2002 and Priem and Hemminger 2012.

authorship and priority, just as Galileo sought to do. Publishers have also provided an endorsement of the works they published with their "brand," which often communicates information about subject matter and quality to potential readers and to promotion and tenure committees; a publication from Oxford University Press means something significantly different from one from a smaller and less distinguished publisher. Libraries have added the preservation and archiving function to these services and have extended the reach of individual works of scholarship well beyond the relatively small numbers who could afford to buy a particular book or subscribe to a journal. Individual scholars, usually academic faculty, have, of course, traditionally provided the content for these books and journals and also, in many cases, done the actual intellectual work of evaluation (peer-reviewing) and editing as volunteers called upon by the publishers.

These functions that are traditionally associated with the publication process—registration, validation, filtration, dissemination, and designation—have provided scholars with great benefits over the years and account for why scholars often still feel great loyalty to publishers and the traditional system of publication. But it is important to recognize the pressures that this system is under. Various factors, including the huge growth in the number of submitted manuscripts over the past forty years, have driven prices for scholarly journals up at a rate much faster than the rate of inflation or the rate at which academic library budgets have grown (Bosch, Henderson, and Klusendorf 2011). Indeed, the fact that library budgets have not been able to keep up with the rising prices of scholarly journals has led to widespread cancellations of subscriptions and also to a startling decrease in the ability of academic libraries to purchase monographs, since an ever-larger percentage of their budgets goes to subscription costs. This has meant that library collections often show a growing bias for the sciences, since these disciplines depend more on journal publication while the humanities in particular still often focus on books. Increasingly, libraries have to consider the degree to which the prices they are paying for journal subscriptions, which are often "bundled" into high-price packages with dozens and even hundreds of titles, actually reflect the value they obtain from these packages.

Even before the age of the Internet, the pressures on academic publishing were clear. In the 1960s, Chester Kerr, the then-director of the Yale University Press, remarked about the publication of scholarly monographs, "We publish the smallest editions at the greatest cost, and on these we place the highest prices, and then try to market them to people who can least afford them. This is madness" (quoted in Hawes 1967, 5). And this assessment predated the situation described above, where academic books are increasingly difficulty for libraries to purchase while journal subscriptions are becoming prohibitively expensive.

In the digital environment, it is harder and harder to correlate value with the cost of traditional journal subscriptions. For one thing, the traditional publishing business model was built on economic scarcity; it was difficult and expensive to print, market, and distribute books, and it required the investment of significant resources. Only a limited number of businesses could amass the needed capital and channels for marketing and distribution. As those businesses were called upon to publish more and more material, prices naturally rose. Capital still must be invested in the process of selecting, editing, and reviewing submissions, but the tasks of printing, marketing, and distribution have changed dramatically. The Internet offers worldwide distribution, lower production costs (although publishers sometimes dispute this), and rapid searchability. In these conditions, purchasers, especially libraries, wonder why the costs for online subscriptions are often as high or higher than they have been for print. Part of the explanation is undoubtedly a different form of scarcity: the artificial scarcity that is created by copyright. Copyright is defined as a limited monopoly, and its intent is to create scarcity where otherwise a work could be copied and distributed quite widely. The purpose of this monopoly is to give authors and creators an incentive to continue to create by supporting a profitable market. The fact that publishers hold the copyrights in most of the works they publish is a significant factor in the ability to charge high prices, especially since the market for academic work is "inelastic"—meaning that one work of scholarship is seldom an adequate substitute for a different work.

The concern over cost, value, and the effects of the copyright monopoly is not limited to libraries. In early 2012, a group of scholars, led by some prominent mathematicians, began an online pledge to boycott Elsevier, the largest of the commercial scholarly publishers. The signers of the pledge, and there were over 11,600 of them in less than a year, assert that they will not submit work to an Elsevier journal nor agree to edit or review for a journal from this publisher (Cost of Knowledge 2014). They cite predatory pricing, bundling policies, and support for legislation that limits open-access options for authors as the reasons for this boycott, which indicates the depth of frustration that scholars themselves are beginning to feel about the traditional mode of scholarly communications.

Digital and online communication obviously changes the conditions for the distribution and consumption of scholarship, as it does for nearly every form of creative or intellectual production. The Budapest Open Access Initiative, discussed below, sums up the situation this way:

> An old tradition and a new technology have converged to make possible an unprecedented public good. The old tradition is the willingness of scientists and scholars to publish the fruits of their research in scholarly journals without payment, for the sake of inquiry and knowledge. The new technology is the Internet. (BOAI 2002)

A great many new options and opportunities are available for scholarly authors. Each new option has advantages as well as challenges and pitfalls. Many of the challenges we face in the digital scholarly environment are problems associated with abundance rather than scarcity. But the degree to which authors will control their choice of publication options is still largely a matter of copyright, and we shall turn next to considering how copyright and control figure into the transition in scholarly communications. But more broadly we want to sketch the advantages and disadvantages associated with each of the new models of disseminating scholarship in order to provide authors and creators with the best framework for deciding which form of distribution, and which form of copyright management, best serves their own individual needs.

Advantages and Disadvantages—Traditional Publication in Subscription-Based Journal

Advantages

- Pre-identified audience of subscribers.
- Established journal branding and impact factor.
- Peer review coordinated by publisher staff.
- Editor-selected contents.
- Copyright managed by publisher.
- Sophisticated indexing and search functions.

Disadvantages

- Toll barrier results in limited audience (not open to all readers).
- Selective and expensive to produce (not open to all authors).
- Large publisher may offer limited attention and resources to one author or single journal.
- No reuse of content, even by author, without permission.
- Limitations on media that can be used or included
- Complex copyright transfers and licensing.

COPYRIGHT AND CONTROL

The idea of a scholarly author retaining copyright in her work after publication, or even being concerned about how the various rights in the copyright "bundle" were divvied up, would not have made much sense before the advent of widespread digital communications. Authors needed to publish their works and were willing to give away their rights under copyright law in order to do so; such rights as they might need to retain, such as the right to reuse an article as a chapter in a longer work by the same author, were handled either by routine contract provisions or by an unwritten understanding that both parties tolerated. Although authors seldom profited from their work, the need for an economically viable enterprise to handle publication was indisputable, since no other options were available.

In the digital environment, things are very different, in part because digital technologies allow creation and dissemination to be separated from the need for economic exclusivity. A single form of distribution, from which an intermediary makes a sufficient profit to support the enterprise, is no longer a necessity. Thus the basic bargain on which the copyright transfer for scholarly works was based no longer seems sensible. This change has exposed a fact that has always been true; people create for a lot of reasons other than to make money. In her book *Digital Copyright*, Jessica Litman (2001, 102) expresses this truth in the form of a growing amazement at "the extraordinary variety and innovativeness of the expression available over the Net that isn't professionally created and formatted commercial content, but that explores some of the new possibilities of the medium."

Some of this expression is academic research and scholarship, and more of it could be. Indeed, the idea that the Internet could be as much a tool for finding knowledge as it is for finding pornography is a very attractive one.[2] Nor should it be difficult to achieve. Indeed, for academic authors, the economic incentives made possible by copyright and the exclusivity that it fosters have never been a significant motive for academic authorship. Scholars simply seldom make money from their intellectual works, and they benefit the most from the widest possible dissemination. But this does not mean that copyright is not important to scholars. On the contrary, the control that copyright ownership bestows on an author is key for maintaining the ability to determine exactly how a work is to be distributed and which of the many options now available will best serve a particular work and the needs of its author.

The rewards for academic authorship come from a system that is entirely separate from, and almost alien to, the economic rewards that are the incentive of commercial creators. The institutions for which academic authors and creators work bestow most of these rewards, and we shall look at the promotion and tenure system in more detail shortly. But for now we can note that some of the rewards that motivate academics are tied to publication via recognized and respected outlets (although none are connected to the actual presence of a subscription fee), while others are more internal and divorced from the form of publication. Indeed, some of the reputational rewards that academic authors covet most are actually harmed by the limited access to scholarly works that is a defining feature of the traditional publication system; only subscribers can have access because that restriction ensures the continued viability of the publication, even though the author almost never shares in its profits. While this limitation makes business sense for the publishers, it is actually harmful to authors, whose reputations, as well as the progress of science and the arts, increase as more people become aware of their work, and it is contrary to the nature of the digital technologies that are rapidly becoming the main form for distributing scholarship.

---

2. It is interesting that the search for new ways to distribute pornography seems to be a significant factor both in technological development and in the making of copyright law for a digital age. The adult entertainment company Perfect 10 has brought several lawsuits that have shaped fair use as it applies online, and the role of the industry in technological advances is detailed in Peter Johnson's (1996) article.

The Internet, to paraphrase a common remark, interprets all forms of access restrictions as damage and builds routes around them. The business of trying to limit access to scholarly resources on the Internet is an endless game of trying to plug leaks and prevent behaviors that are natural to the technology and to the authors and users of the works (Litman 2001, 12–13).

That the exclusivity that copyright is intended to foster is a poor fit with the needs and desires of scholars is demonstrated by a recent phenomenon that would have been unthinkable only a few years ago. Publishers have begun to file copyright infringement lawsuits against universities and faculty members for providing unauthorized access to academic works created by the very system of higher education that is accused of infringement. In a case begun in 2008 and in which the trial phase concluded with a decision supporting fair use, three academic publishers, including two large university presses, sued Georgia State University for infringing the publisher copyrights.[3] They argued that making short excerpts of scholarly works available to students in specific classes, either through the libraries' electronic reserves system or through course pages in a learning management system, was infringing unless a license fee was paid each semester for each excerpt. Over a dozen individual faculty members were cross-examined at trial over their decisions, and the trial court ruling examined each pedagogical decision in detail to determine if it constituted infringement. Only a small number of infringements were found—many uses were determined to be fair use—but the idea of academics being sued over the use of academic works in teaching provided a wake-up call to many about the need to manage copyright in ways that benefit scholarship and not simply leave the matter in the hands of publishers whose interests are necessarily quite different from those of the academy.[4]

---

3. As of this writing, the trial court ruling is being appealed by the publisher plaintiffs.

4. The case of Cambridge University Press et al. v. Patton was tried in the District Court for the Northern District of Georgia, and a massive decision was handed down on May 11, 2012. That decision can be found at http://docs.justia.com/cases/federal/district-courts/georgia/gandce/1:2008cv01425/150651/423.

MANAGING COPYRIGHTS

As these considerations demonstrate, the control over a work that is bestowed with copyright remains important for scholarly authors, even when it is divorced from the incentive to make money. Copyright gives an author options and the opportunity to make decisions about which channels for distribution are most beneficial to that author. On the other hand, relinquishing copyright takes these options away from the author and may even subject her to liability for using her own work and the work of her colleagues who have also surrendered the control that is part of copyright.

In the digital environment, responsible copyright management requires intentional decisions about how to dispose of or retain the rights in copyright. This does not mean that traditional publication is never an appropriate option; indeed, it is still the preferred option for many academic works, especially journal articles, and it will remain so for the foreseeable future. But it is still important for rights holders (the authors) to make careful decisions. If the publisher requires a transfer of copyright, does it make allowances for future uses of the work that may be important to the author, even after copyright is assigned to another? There are diverse possibilities for these future uses, and it is difficult for many scholars to predict what they might want to do with their work, what new options for dissemination and discussion they may want to exploit in an unpredictable technological environment. Nevertheless, these decisions require some foresight, as well as some informed guesswork.

The key for many academic authors to appropriate copyright management is to consider desirable future uses and to make choices for current distribution that does not foreclose these future options. In many cases, this will mean thinking in terms of "traditional publication AND," or "traditional publication AFTER." By this I mean that some authors will elect to publish in traditional subscription journals but also retain the rights necessary to support some additional type of dissemination, like Web archiving of an article. Others will disseminate their work first in more informal channels, such as an academic blog, and then seek to publish the final version after there has been this informal discussion and refinement; this is an increasingly common option for scholarly books.[5]

Two fundamental avenues for copyright management are currently in play for academic authors, and we shall discuss them in turn. The first is attention to publication contracts with traditional publishers. These contracts are often taken for granted, and in previous years that did no harm. But it is now imperative that authors consider the contents of these contracts and negotiate them in ways that will preserve the desired options for disseminating their work. The other channel for copyright management is open-access publishing in its various forms, and we shall consider these forms, and the advantages and disadvantages associated with each, at some length. It is in the context of this latter discussion that we will address the increasingly urgent problem of reforming the promotion and tenure system for academic authors.

THE PUBLICATION CONTRACT

Contracts are powerful legal tools that can determine the course of a relationship between two or more parties. They are often referred to as "private law" arrangements, since private parties can use a contract to fill in gaps left by statutory law or simply override most of the provisions of statutory law, and the courts will, for the most part, enforce those decisions as memorialized in a contract. Two general points are important before we turn to the specifics of contracts for the publication of scholarship. The first is that contracts usually bind only the parties that

---

5.   Two recent books that were developed and disseminated in this way are Siva Vaidhyanathan's (2011) *The Googlization of Everything (and Why We Should Worry)*, which was developed at a blog at www.googlizationofeverything.com (site now discontinued) and subsequently published by the University of California Press and Kathleen Fitzpatrick's (2011) *Planned Obsolescence: Publishing, Technology and the Future of the Academy.*

sign them. While a third party (assuming only two parties have signed the contract) may gain some benefits under an agreement, most of the time only the actual parties have obligations that they must fulfill or risk the legal penalties for breach of contract (which are usually monetary damages paid to the non-breaching party to prevent that party from suffering due to the breach). The other point is that it is perfectly possible to give away rights, by contract, that one would otherwise have under the "default" provisions of local, state, and federal law. For example, in an employment contract, employees often surrender their constitutional right to free speech, at least in regard to certain matters, by agreeing not to publicly criticize or speak on behalf of the employer. The rights that both owners and users of a copyrighted work would otherwise have under the law are likewise subject to modification or elimination through contractual agreement. It is for this reason that attention must be paid to publication contracts, since the uses of a work that can be made after the contract is signed, including uses made by the author (and *former* copyright holder), likely will be entirely governed by the contract.

The "standard" publishing contract—if we can speak of a standard contract in an industry where every publisher and sometimes every journal uses a slightly different agreement—is a transfer or assignment of copyright. These words mean the same thing, which is that copyright as a whole ceases to be held by the author and moves to being owned by the publisher. From that point on, all of the exclusive rights that are afforded as part of copyright belong to the publisher, except insofar as some specific rights are given back to the author by the contract. Under the terms of the copyright law, an assignment or transfer can be accomplished only by a written agreement that is signed by the rights holder (17 U.S.C. § 204(a)).

Most publication contracts allow the author to retain or have back some specific rights to use his or her creation. These retained rights are always quite limited, or else a complete transfer of the exclusive rights would not have been used in the first place. The most common rights that scholarly authors retain are the right to use their own work with students they are teaching without seeking permission; the right to reuse the work in various forms, such as conferences (and conference proceedings), dissertations, or collections of articles written by the same author; and the right to share the work with colleagues on an individual and non-systematic basis. Since even these uncontroversial retained rights are not standardized, it is import for an author who is transferring her copyright to verify the presence of and the scope defined for each of these rights before planning or making subsequent uses of her own authored work.

A majority of publication contracts today also include some language about how an author may make his work available on the Internet, a practice called "self-archiving" that will be discussed again when we consider open-access options. But for now, we need to note three important considerations that are always a part of contract provisions about self-archiving and that an author must be aware of.

First, publication contracts that allow self-archiving nearly always specify what version of an article may be placed on the Web. Three distinct versions are in play in these clauses. The "preprint" of an article is the original completed version that the author wrote and submitted for consideration to the journal. It is the form of the article prior to any changes made after the peer-review process. The practice of making such preprints available on the Web is very common in physics and computer science, using the open-access repository called arXiv, but it is less acceptable to many scholars in other fields, especially in the humanities. The version that most publication contracts allow authors to self-archive is the "post-print," a term which is sometimes treated as synonymous with the author's final version or final manuscript or the "submitted version." This finished version incorporates the changes suggested by the editor and peer reviews; it is the final version that the author sends to the journal for publication, but it does not have the copy-editing and formatting that are part of the journal production process. The version with those production changes, called the published version or the final PDF (which is the format in which most publishers distribute their journals online), is the version authors are allowed to self-archive by only a minority of the publishers that permit this practice; unfortunately, the term *post-print* also sometimes refers to this published PDF.[6] It is far more common to be able to self-archive some form of the "post-print" version of an article than the final version,[7] which sometimes raises an issue for authors who would like to self-archive but are reluctant to have multiple versions of their work on the Internet.

Another restriction that is often placed on the posting of an article by the author to the Internet is the type of website that will host that article. Journal publishers obviously do not want sites that too closely replicate the contents of their own journal databases, so they usually designate that authors may self-archive their articles only on personal websites (such as an author's departmental profile, for example) or one at the institution that employs the author (such as a university's repository of faculty scholarship). Sometimes a "disciplinary" website is allowed; this would include something like the arXiv website for physics already mentioned, or the RePEc (Research Papers in Economics) site that is favored by economists. Often the kind of website that is permitted as a venue for self-archiving is explicitly linked to the version that may be archived. Thus a contract may allow a preprint to be used on the arXiv site but stipulate that the post-print can be used only on a personal or institutional site. Finally, it is worth noting that one major publisher allows authors to self-archive their own published work on "secure internal Web sites," which presumably means password-protected sites accessible only to the university community. This provision allows the free use of faculty articles in teaching and sharing

---

6. The Sherpa RoMEO database about self-archiving policies of various publishers uses the term *post-print* in regard to both the final manuscript and the published PDF. There is a list on the RoMEO site, however, which tells authors which journals actually allow self-archiving of the published PDF, found at www.sherpa.ac.uk/romeo/PDFandIR.html.

7. In a recent study that is not yet published but that was shared with the author, David Hansen of the University of California, Berkeley Law School found that roughly 20 percent of scientific journals allowed self-archiving of the final PDF version, while almost 50 percent allowed only the post-print to be used. See also SHERPA/RoMEO 2014.

between colleagues at the same institution, but it does not allow the author to reach the broader audience that is usually the goal of self-archiving.

A third consideration that is sometimes built into contractual provisions governing self-archiving is an embargo. Some publishers will not permit an author whose work they are publishing to self-archive at all until some period of time has elapsed after the date of publication. These embargo periods range from six months to two years, although the most common embargo period, when one is imposed, seems to be one year.

Another form of Internet distribution that publication contracts usually deal with is the archiving of articles for public access that is increasingly required by bodies that fund scientific research. These "funder mandates" are imposed on researchers when they are given grants for research and generally require that a post-print of any peer-reviewed and published articles that arise from the funded research be made available on the open Web after some embargo period. They may also impose requirements about how the data that underlies the reported research must be managed. The Wellcome Trust and the Howard Hughes Medical Institute both build such mandates into their grant agreements, and authors must be sure that their publication contracts allow them to comply with commitments they have undertaken as a condition of funding. The most ubiquitous of the public access mandates, however, is that imposed by the US National Institutes of Health (NIH), which requires all articles that arise from NIH-funded research be made publicly available (to everyone, not just subscribers to a specific journal) in a database called PubMed Central within twelve months of publication (NIH 2014). Many journal publishers now submit articles to PMC on behalf of authors, and they almost always take advantage of the twelve-month delay in public accessibility. But if a publisher does not comply automatically with the NIH requirement, it is incumbent on authors who have received NIH funding to notify their publisher and determine that their contract specifies that compliance will not breach the agreement and informs the author of what embargo period to request. In these cases, actual submission to the PMC database will be the author's responsibility, and if NIH-funded authors cannot modify their publication contracts so as to allow this PMC deposit, they must seek a different publisher.

Publication contracts are always drafted by the publisher and presented to authors, but they are negotiable. The first step for an author concerned about the rights she is retaining (and all authors should be concerned about that) is to read the relevant sections of the contract carefully to see if the needs that she foresees for herself and her work are already addressed. If some need or needs are not addressed in the contract, the best next step may simply be to ask the publisher if it can be written in; this technique is successful in a surprising number of cases, although those where it is not get more attention. Where the problem an author sees with a publication contract is not what it leaves out but something unacceptable to the author that is included, she can try to simply line out the provision or phrase and see if the publisher will still accept the contract. It is important to realize that if a contract simply does not address a particular issue, that silence leaves in place the normal rights, rules, limitations, and exceptions that are delineated by copyright law.

One tool that some authors employ when negotiating contracts is the so-called "author addendum," which is a short provision drafted for authors to attach to their publication contracts in order to retain some uniform designated right, usually a broad right for self-archiving, along with other noncommercial teaching and research uses. These addenda are available from a variety of sources—sometimes universities or consortia of universities draft them for their authors to use, and the advocacy group known as SPARC (Scholarly Publishing and Academic Resources Coalition), formed by the Association of Research Libraries, offers a very popular set of such addenda, adaptable for different needs.[8] These addenda seem to meet with mixed success; some publishers say they will reject submitted addenda as a matter of policy, while scholars in certain disciplines report good success using addenda (see Fowler 2012). Even

---

8.   The SPARC addenda can be found at SPARC 2007. A list of author addenda is maintained by the Open Access Directory (OAD 2012).

where an addendum is rejected or never submitted, it can serve a purpose because it helps authors consider which rights it is most important for them to retain. Thus an addendum can be a helpful tool for understanding the contract presented and deciding whether or not there are additional rights that the author wants to retain. Even when an addendum is rejected, the author can still ask for the desired rights on a more personal level; some success has been reported using that technique.

In addition to the contested issue of author rights retention, there are a few other clauses that may be found in publication contracts that might be problematic for scholarly authors. Some clauses that sound important may be relatively benign; a "force majeure" clause, for example, simply gives both parties leeway in the event that performance of the contract is impeded by circumstances that the parties cannot control, such as a natural disaster. But other clauses should be understood and carefully considered by anyone who is signing a publication contract. A clause called a "merger clause" or "entire agreement," for example, states that any promises made or decisions reached prior to the contract being signed are not enforceable if they are not included in the document. This may be very significant if an author is hoping to rely on oral assurances made by an editor; such reliance will be misplaced if the contract contains a merger clause (as nearly all do) and the promises are not written in. Many contracts also include warranties and indemnification clauses in which the author makes certain promises, such as that her work is original and not libelous of anyone, and promises to pay for the defense of any claims made against the publisher on those matters. These clauses are, again, quite standard, but it is important to examine their scope to be sure they do not go too far in creating author liability for things he or she may not be able to control.

Many contracts contain a provision that assures an author that his name will always be associated with the work whenever the publisher distributes it. Often this clause says that the author's "moral right of attribution" has been asserted. Most countries recognize such a moral right for an author to always have attribution for her work, but US copyright law does not. Therefore US authors may especially want to include this provision, since it is only by contract that their right of attribution can be safeguarded.

Finally, authors should beware of "non-compete" clauses in which an author promises not to publish anything in some future period of time that might compete with the publication being governed by the contract. Non-compete clauses are common in the employment arena, and courts have held that they must be reasonably limited as to the time and geographic area in which competition is forbidden. But for scholarly authors they raise additional concerns, since a scholar's work is always cumulative, and publication of the next stage of one's research may often appear to compete with previous publications. Derivative works, such as a slide presentation based on an article, may also seem problematic if the author agrees to such a provision. These clauses are nearly always unnecessary in scholarly publication contracts, except, perhaps, when a textbook is being published, and they are excellent candidates for deletion before the author signs and returns the contract.

Once an acceptable contract has been negotiated, it should be signed by the appropriate parties. When more than one author has written a work, it is often best that each author sign the publication contract. It is true that each co-author can exercise the rights under copyright without the consent of the others, but this is a recipe for later conflict. It is far better to have all of the authors reach agreement about the contract and then sign it; in some cases the publisher may insist on this. But having all parties sign may be a problem for scientific papers, where a great many researchers are often involved and may be listed as authors. The tradition of a "corresponding author"—a person designated to handle relations with the publisher, peer-reviewers, and others who wish to contact the research team—addresses this problem. A difficulty could arise, however, if the corresponding author is not actually a legal author in terms of copyright law—one who has actually contributed protectable expression to the article. Since contracts are so often transfers of copyright, the person signing on behalf of a research team really should be a copyright holder. Thus having a graduate student or postdoc who worked on the research but wrote no part of the article serve as the corresponding author is not a good idea.

Another difficulty may arise in the situation where a publisher tries to use a "click-through" online contract instead of a document. The trend in courts is to enforce these contracts, but they should not be acceptable to scholarly authors because they are not negotiable. They also may run afoul of the explicit requirement in the law that a copyright transfer be "signed." The best course when confronted with a click-through publication agreement is to insist on a written version that will override the online contract, even if agreement to the latter is required to complete the submission process.

OPEN ACCESS DEFINED

A simple and useful definition of open access can be easily stated; it refers to the online availability of scholarly works in a form that is free from access restrictions (such as subscription fees) and restrictions on use (such as copyright or technological protection measures). This definition is derived from more complex statements that were formulated by three international meetings, held in 2001 and 2003, of scholars who were seeking to define how the Internet could provide a major step forward in advancing the efficiency, utility, and impact of scientific research. Each definition was named after the location of the meeting, so we often hear references to the Budapest Open Access Initiative, the Berlin Declaration on Open Access to Knowledge in the Sciences and Humanities, and the Bethesda Statement on Open Access Publishing. The core definition from each of these statements is provided in the example below.[9]

The reasons these gatherings of scholars were so committed to using the Internet to improve access to scholarly literature have to do with the advantages associated with such access. First, and probably most

---

9.   For the complete text of these statements and a discussion of their implications and importance, see Crawford 2011. Another important source, which is itself openly accessible, is Suber 2012.

important, open access improves the speed and quality of scientific research. Because articles can be posted and accessed much more quickly than traditional publication cycles allow, more and more scientists rely on openly available work as the core of their research processes. A 2012 report prepared for the Committee on Economic Development listed four specific benefits for scientific research from public access to research results, benefits that the report concluded outweighed any potential costs:

1. Accelerated progress due to the increased speed and greater diffusion of knowledge.
2. Greater diversity among the researchers able to approach a problem and more opportunity to explore different research paths.
3. More follow-on research.
4. Continuing evaluation of research and improved accountability. (Maxwell 2012, 6)

Another important consideration is the social benefit associated with open access; the public availability of research literature, especially in the health sciences, offers an opportunity for nonacademic readers to find material that can be vitally important to them. Such readers can be patients seeking medical information, researchers, clinicians or aid workers in the developing world, or even policy makers who lack ready access to scholarly literature. For example, when the Duke University faculty adopted an open-access policy for its scholarly journal output, it was compelling for them to hear about a Duke student who was serving as a Congressional intern during the 2009 health care debate and how his ability to consult expensive databases of research literature (because of his status as a student at a university with many such subscription) became important to legislative aides who lacked his degree of access.[10]

---

10. The author was present at this discussion in March 2010.

There are also benefits for individual scholars when their work is made available in some form of open access. Because it is accessible to many times more potential readers, there is a greater likelihood of having a substantial impact on one's field of study. Repeated studies have shown that open access articles have a "citation advantage," as well as a readership advantage, over those that are accessible only to subscribers.[11]

Open Access Definitions

Budapest
By "open access" to this literature, we mean its free availability on the public internet, permitting any users to read, download, copy, distribute, print, search, or link to the full texts of these articles, crawl them for indexing, pass them as data to software, or use them for any other lawful purpose, without financial, legal, or technical barriers other than those inseparable from gaining access to the internet itself. The only constraint on reproduction and distribution, and the only role for copyright in this domain, should be to give authors control over the integrity of their work and the right to be properly acknowledged and cited. (BOIA 2002)

Berlin
Open access contributions must satisfy two conditions:

1. The author(s) and right holder(s) of such contributions grant(s) to all users a free, irrevocable, worldwide, right of access to, and a license to copy, use, distribute, transmit and display the work publicly and to make and distribute derivative works, in any digital medium for any responsible purpose, sub-

11. Among many studies, see Gargouri et al 2010; Zhang 2006; Davis 2011. Steve Hitchcock (2013) offers an annotated bibliography of a large number of these "citation advantage" studies.

ject to proper attribution of authorship (community standards, will continue to provide the mechanism for enforcement of proper attribution and responsible use of the published work, as they do now), as well as the right to make small numbers of printed copies for their personal use.

2. A complete version of the work and all supplemental materials, including a copy of the permission as stated above, in an appropriate standard electronic format is deposited (and thus published) in at least one online repository using suitable technical standards (such as the Open Archive definitions) that is supported and maintained by an academic institution, scholarly society, government agency, or other well-established organization that seeks to enable open access, unrestricted distribution, inter operability, and long-term archiving. ("Berlin Declaration" 2003)

Bethesda
An Open Access Publication[1] is one that meets the following two conditions:

1. The author(s) and copyright holder(s) grant(s) to all users a free, irrevocable, worldwide, perpetual right of access to, and a license to copy, use, distribute, transmit and display the work publicly and to make and distribute derivative works, in any digital medium for any responsible purpose, subject to proper attribution of authorship[2], as well as the right to make small numbers of printed copies for their personal use.

2. A complete version of the work and all supplemental materials, including a copy of the permission as stated above, in a suitable standard electronic format is deposited immediately upon initial publi-

cation in at least one online repository that is supported by an academic institution, scholarly society, government agency, or other well-established
organization that seeks to enable open access,
unrestricted distribution, interoperability, and
long-term archiving (for the biomedical sciences,
PubMed Central is such a repository).

Notes:
1. Open access is a property of individual works, not necessarily journals or publishers.
2. Community standards, rather than copyright law, will continue to provide the mechanism for enforcement of proper attribution and responsible use of the published work, as they
do now. (Brown et al., 2003)

Because citations translate into greater impact on a particular field of
study, the prospect of more readers who will have faster access is a primary driver when authors decide to publish their work in an open-access
format. Obviously a higher citation rate is important for the promotion
and tenure processes that most scholarly authors must undergo. It is often
necessary, however, to remind promotion and tenure committees that
most forms of open-access publication are fully compatible with peer
review; the advantage of higher citation rates is available only once such
committees overcome the prejudice, increasingly uncommon it seems,
that open-access publications are not peer-reviewed or are simply "vanity" publications. We will look more closely at how different open-access
models are related to peer review in a moment.

One other advantage of open access that is related to this increase in
readers and citations is the ability to track impact on a more granular,
article-specific level. Traditional publication has the advantage of a well-
defined method for measuring impact, the journal impact factor. These
"metrics" are easily available and are well understood by officials responsi-

ble for promotion and tenure. But impact factors are related to a journal as a whole and cannot tell us much about the specific impact of a particular article. When articles are available online, more article-level metrics are available, and the more open access to the article is, the more various the opportunities for measuring these forms of access become. Thus there is a significant movement to explore alternative metrics or "altmetrics," that can give scholars, and those who evaluate them, access to more specific information about how often an article has been accessed, downloaded, or cited (see Priem et al. 2011). The citation rates can be tracked not only for other online and open-access publications, but also for more informal, but for many disciplines increasingly important, modes of citation in blogs and Web-based discussions. The alternative metrics are a burgeoning new opportunity for scholars to get a fuller picture of the actual impact that they are having on a field, rather than allowing a journal impact factor to serve as an imperfect surrogate for that influence. One issue that will arise around these types of measures, however, is whether there is a danger that multiple outlets will syphon off citations into different silos of influence that could raise the level of complexity involved in accurately assessing impact. Several projects in the field are working on altmetrics in general and this difficulty in particular, and some disciplinary repositories are making it possible to automate the process of coordinating the collection of download statistics from multiple repositories.[12]

OPEN-ACCESS OPTIONS AND PEER REVIEW

As has already been noted, most forms of open access to scholarly journal articles are fully compatible with traditional peer-reviewed publication in a scholarly journal. The three most generally recognized methods of

12. Altmetric.com (www.altmetric.com) is a service that offers to collect citation demographics from multiple sources for scholarly authors. The economics repository RePEc (http://repec.org), for example, has a citation analysis tool called CitEc, as well as an API that facilitates the consolidation of OA article statistics.

disseminating an article openly—publication in an open-access journal, publication in a traditional journal that offers a "hybrid" model to make selected articles openly accessible, and self-archiving of a traditionally published article in an institutional or disciplinary repository—all involve peer review managed through a publisher. In this section we will examine the first two of these models, then turn in the final section to self-archiving as well as more informal and direct forms of Web dissemination.

Open-Access Journals

Publishing in an entirely open-access journal, one that is freely available online so that anyone with an Internet connection can read all of its contents, is often called the "gold road" to open access. It is an increasingly common choice for scholars, especially because a number of open-access journals are rapidly gaining good reputations and high-impact metrics. For scholars who opt to take this gold road to open access, the benefits of open access are often combined with publication in a recognized and respected journal, which is important in the promotion and tenure process. But scholars who wish to publish in gold open-access journals need to understand some of the variations in the way these journals are funded and beware of unethical practices that sometimes besmirch a largely reputable segment of the publishing industry.

Broadly speaking, these fully open-access journals are funded in one of two ways. Either the cost of publishing the journal is wholly underwritten by some agency or institution, or else the journal is supported by charging authors a fee either upon submission of an article, in which case the fee should be quite low to account for the fact that many articles will not be accepted and will need to be submitted elsewhere, or after an article is accepted but prior to publication (when the fee is usually higher).

Complete support by an institution is actually a very common open-access business model. Many smaller journals are now supported by academic libraries, which use an open source platform to facilitate the editorial and peer-review processes and publish the journal. Since the editors and reviewers are volunteers (as they are with traditional journals as well), the costs for supporting such journals are not high, requiring primarily stable server space and some low level of technical support. A number of small but respected journals that have previously been managed independently by faculty members or by small societies have made the move to this form of publication; examples include *Greek, Roman, and Byzantine Studies*, hosted by the Duke University Libraries (http://grbs.library.duke.edu) and *Disability Studies Quarterly*, which is hosted by the Ohio State University Libraries (http://dsq-sds.org).

Institutions are also supporting other much larger and less specialized projects in open-access publishing so that neither readers nor authors have to pay for the publication. In 2011, a very ambitious journal called *eLife* was announced; it will be funded by three major biomedical research funders, the Wellcome Trust, the Howard Hughes Medical Institute, and the Max Planck Society. *eLife* is explicitly intended to rival such highly respected general science titles as *Nature* and *Science*. The intention is that *eLife* will always be open-access, and no author-side fees have been charged during its first three years. This period is intended to give time for *eLife* to develop a reputation and a readership and to see how the whole area of open-access publishing develops over that time.[13] It seems likely that, with its sponsorship by well-known research agencies and its highly respected editorial board, *eLife* has laid a solid foundation to become a successful and respected venue for scientific publications.

The second model—sometimes inaccurately called "author pays"—is the way the best known open-access journals, such as those published by BioMed Central or the Public Library of Science, are funded, but it is not the dominant one.[14] This model, primarily where fees are charged

---

13. Interview with Mark Patterson, one of the founders of eLife, at http://www.researchinformation.info/features/feature.php?feature_id=477.

14. According to an extensive study by Harvard professor Stuart Shieber (2009), approximately 70 percent of open-access journals do not charge any author-side fee or APC. Thus the common belief that APCs are the dominant form of support for OA journals is incorrect.

after acceptance of an article, can legitimately be called "author-side" support even though the fees are most commonly paid through grant funds or by an institution rather than directly by the author. The fees are usually referred to as "article-processing charges" (APCs), and they replace subscription income, so they make open access to the contents of these journals possible, but they are not, in most cases, payments made in order to get an article into the journal. This is an important distinction between fully open-access journals and so-called "vanity" publications; most "author-side" open-access journals, and certainly the best known ones, carry out a peer-review process comparable to that done for more traditional journals. Since most peer review is done by scholars employed elsewhere and serving as volunteers, rigorous review of submissions is not incompatible with the relatively lower costs associated with these open-access journals.

We can focus on the two publishers mentioned above to more fully explore the way open-access journals work. BioMed Central (BMC) was begun independently but has been purchased by the large publisher Springer; it continues to be run as a separate set of journals, most of which are supported by article-processing charges. Some of these journals have developed significant impact factors in the ten years and more that they have been published. *BMC Genomics* and *BMC Evolutionary Biology*, for example, are both ranked, by impact factor, among the leading journals in their subdisciplines, while the more general *BMC Medicine* has achieved an impact factor of over six (which means that articles in that journal are cited an average of six times a year, a very respectable number for a specialized field [BMC 2014]). The article-processing charges for BMC journals are currently set at around $2,300.

The Public Library of Science, or PLOS, also publishes journals that are well-respected in their fields. PLOS has seven discipline-specific journals, in biology, genetics, computational biology, and medicine. These journals, like those from BMC, are peer-reviewed and enjoy high impact factors; *PLOS Biology*, in fact, is currently the highest impact journal in the field.

Another journal from the same organization, called *PLOS ONE*, is taking a different approach to publishing scientific research. Submissions to *PLOS ONE* are reviewed, but to a different standard than many other journals; instead of seeking the research articles that will be most important or most interesting to the widest audience, *PLOS ONE* evaluates articles only for scientific validity. Its goal is to publish valid research quickly and inexpensively. The volume of research being published in *PLOS ONE* is impressive; in 2011, one of every sixty articles indexed in the PubMed index were from *PLOS ONE* ("*PLOS ONE*" 2014). The speed of publication it provides, the apparatus for post-publication commentary, and its outsized impact make *PLOS ONE* an increasingly popular publication choice for research scientists.

The article-processing charge for *PLOS ONE* is $1,350 as of this writing, while the fees for publication in the more traditional PLOS journals range from $2,250 to $2,900. Other gold open-access journals, such as those from Hindawi or Frontiers in Research, tend to have slightly lower fees, often in the range of $1,000 to $1,500, and at the moment, the reputation and impact of these publishers is also not as developed.

Because these APCs for publication in fully open-access journals are paid on the submission side, authors are understandably seeking sources to fund their articles when they select one of these gold OA journals. A recent survey suggests that only a small minority of authors, about 12 percent, actually pay these fees from their own funds.[15] Two primary sources are developing as gold OA gains in popularity. When research is funded by a granting agency, those funds often are used to pay APCs. Many granters now permit the use of these funds for this purpose, accept grant budgets that include them, and sometimes insist that OA publishing be included in the proposed budget for a grant proposal. Much research, however, is either not supported by grants or is in a field, like mathematics, where grants are traditionally quite small and it is difficult to find the

---

15. For the article and accompanying data from the Study of Open Access Publishing (SOAP), see Dallmeier-Tiessen et al. 2011.

$2,000 or so that would be needed for gold OA publishing of even a single article. The lack of grant money, and the perception, probably erroneous, that the gold road is the only way for quality scholarship to be published in open access, may account for the much slower uptake of open-access publishing in the humanities (and, to some extent, the social sciences).

In order to counter this difficulty and to encourage what is widely perceived to be the most sustainable alternative to traditional, subscription-based publishing, a number of academic institutions are now managing funds to help support gold OA publishing by their faculty authors. There is a coalition of institutions that have committed themselves to provide such funding, which is called the Compact for Open Access Publishing Equity, or COPE. The members of COPE and some other institutions have set aside funds that will underwrite all or part of the APCs required when faculty wish to publish in these gold open-access journals. Each school decides how much money to earmark for this purpose and what the criteria and procedures for obtaining support will be. But in each case, these funds represent a commitment by research institutions to help authors select the best model for publishing their research and to encourage open access when it is the author's choice.

Unlike subscription charges, which are paid primarily by libraries with a good deal of experience in acquiring scholarly publications, APCs are paid by individual researchers who may lack such expertise. Therefore, they have offered to some unscrupulous "publishers" a new opportunity for abuse. There are certainly some individuals and companies that claim to run open-access journals but that are exclusively interested in collecting APCs and not in managing a quality peer-review process or publishing a sustainable journal. These "predatory" open-access journals have attracted a good deal of attention, but it is important to realize that such practices have always existed on the fringes of academic publishing. Journals that list well-known figures as editors without their knowledge or consent, that cut corners on peer review or that publish biased work because some commercial interest will pay to have it disseminated, have always existed in the subscription-based publishing world, and librarians have formal criteria and informal networks to help them prevent wasting the funds that are entrusted to them. In the gold OA world, researchers need to apply similar techniques to avoid giving their scarce research funds to unscrupulous online publishers. Determining if a journal is listed in the Directory of Open Access Journals (http://doaj.org) or if the publisher is a member of the Open Access Scholarly Publishers Association (http://oaspa.org) is a good first step. Checking to see if a potential OA venue has a recognized impact factor, how many articles it has published, or even if it is known among one's colleagues can also be advantageous.

The online environment tends to level various information sources; the website of a Holocaust denial organization may looks as polished and respectable as that of a noted scientific research center. This does not mean that predatory practices are exclusively an online or open-access problem, but it does mean that the traditional warning "buyer, beware" is particularly applicable in the gold open-access publishing sector. Where in the past the decision about which journals were worth their subscription fees were made in libraries, now decisions about which gold OA journals are worth the APCs they charge must be made by individual authors. Sometimes an author may even choose to publish in a less-than-reputable journal for the advantages that open access has over traditional publishing; in addition to the speed of publication, the online environment allows the publication of lots of small, very specialized niche journals, which can be problematic but also sometimes offers a desirable context for the author. Authors should make this decision advisedly, if they are going to make it at all, and should at least determine that real peer review will take place and that the target journal has published some articles. For most authors, the best course is to seek out those open-access journals in their fields that are known and respected by colleagues; in those venues the advantages of open access can best be combined with the traditional values that have long been associated with the majority of scholarly publishers.

Before we leave the topic of gold open access, we should acknowledge that the models for supporting such publications are not at all settled. While we have focused on the two most common—institutional support and article-processing fees—new experiments are underway that might displace these business practices with something we cannot now imagine. The recently announced journal called *PeerJ* (https://peerj.com) is one example of such an experiment. This unique undertaking is planning to offer "memberships" in the journal to individual researchers, and a membership allows publication in one of two journals. One will be a peer-reviewed journal similar to *PLOS ONE*, and the other will be a "preprint" journal that will allow "crowd-sourced" assessment of the papers. The lifetime memberships, as announced, will begin at $129 for a single publication each year and go up to $259 for a membership that allows unlimited publications. It is far too early to know if this will be a successful plan, although it has been founded by some experienced OA publishers, but it is indicative of the ferment that is currently going on in the area of scholarly communications in general, and open-access publication specifically. These uncertainties and experiments may indicate confusion to some and cause fear, but to many they are exciting hints about the different world ahead of us for disseminating the results of scholarly research.

"Gold" Open Access—Publication in Wholly Open-Access Journal

Advantages

- Open to all readers.
- Peer review managed by publisher staff.
- Journal branding and impact factor being developed.
- Author keeps copyright.
- Editor-selected contents.

- Reuse by users MAY be more clearly defined (as with a CC license), so articles are open to text mining and other, as yet unanticipated uses.
- May be more searchable (Google).
- Indexing and search functionality usually well developed.

Disadvantages

- Cost, in some cases, to author, funder, or institution.
- Reputation (brand) sometimes less developed due to recent establishment.

Hybrid Publications

An increasing number of traditional, subscription-based publishers now offer authors an option to pay an article-processing charge and have their article, and only their article, made immediately available in openly accessible form. Because these journals, including those published by Oxford, Elsevier, and other major firms, are primarily accessible only through subscriptions but have specific articles that are open-access owing to a decision by the author to pay an APC, we call these "hybrid" publications. In some ways, this form of publication seems very reassuring to scholarly authors; they are able to publish in academic titles that are very familiar to them and can also, they believe, realize the benefits of open access by selecting this option offered by the publisher. From the publisher's side, of course, this is an attractive model because it creates a second revenue stream, through APCs, without endangering the subscription income that is the primary means of support for most traditional publishers. In spite of these apparent advantages, these hybrid models have some significant pitfalls for authors.

One obvious drawback of these hybrid models is, of course, cost. Publishers that are using this approach often try to suggest that fee-based OA is the only viable open-access alternative. But as we have already seen, and will see even more clearly when we discuss self-archiving, this is not true. Article-processing charges are one option, but not by any means the only way for an author to get the benefit of open access. And with these hybrid models, the APCs tend to be considerably higher than they are for gold OA journals that charge APCs. The Oxford Open option for Oxford University Press, for example, costs $3,000 for each article, more than twice the cost of gold OA in *PLOS ONE*. These publishers that are experimenting with hybrid open access are, of course, large organizations whose costs, still rooted in printed journals, are quite high, so it is not surprising that they should feel the need for a high APC to replace "lost" subscription costs. It is not clear, however, that these random and occasional OA articles actually do lead to lost subscription revenue; most libraries, for example, will not cancel a subscription simply because some of the articles can be accessed for free. Nor is it clear if these publishers will really follow through on their promise to reduce subscription costs for an institution based on the number of authors from that institution that opt for fee-based OA.

Nevertheless, the author who selects this route will make her articles more available; she will, theoretically, benefit from the citation advantage and the possibility of being discovered by unexpected readers. But even here there is a difficulty. These articles are generally accessible only on the publisher's own website, on which the majority of the articles are behind a subscription wall. Potential readers who do not have subscriptions must either know that a particular article is freely available or take the random chance, by going to that website, that something they are interested in will be freely available. And these open-access articles may be harder to find through search engines since these publisher websites may not be crawled by such tools because the material is generally not available to searchers, although it is growing more common for publisher websites to be crawled and indexed by Google Scholar, at least. And authors who select a hybrid open-access option can improve the discoverability of their article simply by linking to it from their own web page or that of their academic department or institution.

Once a reader does find an open-access article on a publisher's website, one advantage he usually has is that there is a clear statement about what he can do with the article he has found. One of the distinctions that is often made about open access is the difference between *free* meaning without cost (sometimes called "gratis") and *free* meaning available for use without many of the restrictions imposed by copyright (called "libre").[16] This distinction is suggested by the definitions of open access that are discussed above, which refer to open access as freedom from both price barriers and use restrictions. The latter type of freedom is usually accomplished with some kind of license that tells users what they can do with an article—whether they can merely read it, print it out, use it for commercial research, or even create a derivative work from it. Publishers who publish gold or hybrid OA articles are usually good at informing users about what they can do with the open-access articles; indeed, one of the largest OA publishers, Springer, recently announced that all of its OA content would be available under a Creative Commons attribution-only license (this type of license is discussed in detail in chapters 4 and 6), which allows any use as long as the original article is properly cited (Springer 2012). Such a clear statement about how users may use the works that they access is a major advantage of at least some pure gold OA and hybrid models.

One misunderstanding about hybrid open access should be cleared up before we move to other forms of open access. Occasionally we hear from researchers who are funded by the National Institutes of Health that they believe they need to pay for hybrid open access with their publishers in order to comply with the NIH mandate for public access. Sometimes it even seems that representatives of the journals in which they are publishing tell them this, but it is incorrect. The NIH public access mandate requires that works that result from funded research be made available in a specific database called PubMed Central. Open access in some other form is neither required nor sufficient to comply with the mandate. And publishers, even

---

16. For a detailed examination of this terminology, see Suber 2008.

those that have a hybrid open-access option, usually provide another route for NIH compliance; either they work directly with the NIH to see to it that funded articles are deposited in PubMed Central, as Elsevier does, or else they write into their publications contracts a license back to the author that permits compliance. So while PubMed Central deposit is required for all authors whose articles arise from NIH-funded research, NIH compliance does not require that authors pay for hybrid OA when publishing with a traditional publisher that offers that option. Indeed, neither hybrid nor gold OA publishing is itself sufficient to comply with the NIH mandate, which requires something that looks much more like self-archiving.[17]

Hybrid Open-Access Publication with Traditional Publisher

Advantages

- Pre-identified audience.
- Established journal branding and impact factor.
- Peer review managed by publisher staff.
- Editor-selected contents.
- Open to all readers.
- Author retains copyright.
- Indexing and search functionality usually well-developed.

Disadvantages

- Cost to author, funder, or institution.

17. A comprehensive list of NIH policies from academic publishers compiled by the Open Access Directory concludes that "to the best of our knowledge, no publishers anywhere refuse to publish NIH-funded authors on the grounds of the NIH public-access policy. Every publisher we've examined to date offers some way to accommodate NIH-funded authors, even if the method of accommodation is not expressly stated in the copyright transfer agreement. In the rare cases when the copyright transfer does not expressly accommodate NIH-funded authors, publishers who learn that authors must comply with the NIH policy always offer options to make that compliance possible" (see OAD 2013).

- Duplicative costs (institution pays for subscription and often pays publication fee).
- Reuse rights (e.g., text mining) will be defined by publisher.
- Complex licensing, which will vary between different articles in same journal.
- Selective and expensive to produce.
- Publisher may offer limited attention to single author or journal.
- Readers (nonsubscribers to journal) may not find individual OA articles or discern easily which articles they have access to.

SELF-ARCHIVING AND DIRECT WEB PUBLICATION
Self-Archiving

Self-archiving is by far the most common way in which open access to scholarship is accomplished. It refers specifically to making one's own works available on the Internet on a personal website, an institutional repository, or a disciplinary-focused repository maintained outside of one's own institutional domain. These arrangements usually involve peer-reviewed journal articles that have first been published in a scholarly journal and are subsequently posted to a web page or deposited in a repository by the author. Such posting or deposit depends, at least in theory, on the author of the article having retained sufficient rights, or having had those rights licensed back to her after a transfer of copyright. Increasingly, publication contracts are very specific about exactly what forms of self-archiving are and are not permitted to an author; in other words, they parse very carefully the rights that they allow authors to retain or that they license back (publication contracts may use either expression; they usually mean the same thing, although the language of "licensing back" is more accurate). In practice, authors do sometimes self-archive, especially by posting to a personal website, regardless of the specific language in publication contracts. Such actions are technically a breach of contract and copyright infringement, although the likelihood that a publisher would take legal action against the author who had transferred the copyright to it in the first place is small.[18] When an institution manages a repository, usually the university or college library, it tends to be very careful to avoid posting articles without observing the specific contractual terms to which the author originally agreed.

The specific terms in contractual agreements that control where, when, and how an author may self-archive her own work are discussed above, in the subsection of this chapter on publication agreements, so they need not be rehashed here. The three principal stipulations often placed on the rights retained or licensed back to authors for the purpose of self-archiving—rules about the version that may be used, the type of repository in which that version of an article may be placed, and any period of time that must elapse before open access to the article is possible—are the principal ways by which publishers seek to prevent self-archiving from becoming a threat, or a perceived threat, to their subscription income.

Although publishers routinely complain that self-archiving poses a threat to the subscription model publishing business, there is no convincing evidence as of this writing that that is in fact the case. The best studies of library cancellations, and libraries are the major customers for journal and journal package subscriptions, show that open access to self-archived versions of articles is very seldom a reason for such cancellations. For example, a major study by the Publishers Communication Group found that four reasons—low usage, price increases, faculty recommendations, and duplicate print and electronic subscriptions—accounted for over 60

---

18. Although there have been a few well-publicized demands that universities remove final published versions of articles published by Elsevier and the American Society of Civil Engineering from the websites of the article authors, this author knows of no litigation regarding this usage directed against academic authors.

percent of cancellations, while open access was mentioned in less than 5 percent of responses.[19]

One particular form of self-archiving that has publishers especially concerned is what is sometimes called "mandated" self-archiving. This refers to situations where an author is required or strongly encouraged to self-archive his articles, often in a specific repository, after the article has been published in a traditional (or gold open-access) form. These open-access mandates originate from two possible sources, the funding body that supports the research upon which the article is based or the institution that employs the author.

In the United States, the most prominent funder mandate for open access comes from the National Institutes of Health, which is the largest supporter of biomedical research in the nation.[20] According to rules adopted in 2008, all research articles that arise from funded research and are accepted for publication in a peer-reviewed journal must be made publicly accessible in a repository called PubMed Central (PMC) no later than twelve months after publication.[21] Authors are required to deposit their articles in the PMC repository (and to have retained the right to do so) immediately upon acceptance (unless the journal has an agreement with the NIH to do this on behalf of authors), although public access can be delayed. The NIH enforces this mandate by requiring that article numbers assigned by the PMC repository be included in subsequent reports on the use of grant funds, in renewal requests, and on later grant applications.[22]

19. For a report on this study, which covered cancellations made between 2006 and 2011, see PCG 2011. An overview of the evidence regarding the causes (and non-causes) of journal cancellation can be found in Suber 2012, chapter 8.

20. In February 2013, the White House announced a directive to a larger group of federal agencies that sponsor research to prepare plans for similar public access mandates. See Stebbins 2013.

21. The PubMed Central repository (www.ncbi.nlm.nih.gov/pmc) is fully open for public access to all of its contents. It should not be confused with PubMed (www.ncbi.nlm.nih.gov/pubmed), which is a citation database and provides access to the full text of an article only in some cases, where that article has otherwise been made open.

22. The NIH provides a detailed explanation of its policy, along with an FAQ, at NIH 2014.

Because the NIH requires self-archiving in its own repository, the issue of additional payment does not arise. Some funders, however, do ask the authors whose research they support to either self-archive or publish in a gold open-access journal. These funders, including the Wellcome Trust and the Howard Hughes Medical Institute, allow grant funds to be used to pay article-processing charges. The NIH grants also allow such charges in cases where the author prefers an open-access journal, but that does not excuse the requirement of deposit in PubMed Central as well.

The other form of open-access policy should probably not be called a mandate. These are policies for open access adopted by faculties at colleges or universities. Such policies usually take the form of a license granted by all faculty authors to the institution to allow deposit on their behalf in an institutional repository. In every case of which this author is aware, such policies can be waived by the faculty author, so while they reset the default position to open access, they are not true mandates in the sense of being inescapable. These policies are adopted by a faculty body, either an entire institutional faculty or a disciplinary or school faculty within an institution, and are therefore self-imposed. Where an entire university faculty adopts such a policy, it usually becomes part of the faculty handbook and is therefore a condition of employment. Nevertheless, these policies routinely include a waiver provision that allows the faculty member, but not any subsequent rights holder, to opt out of the policy. This is sometimes necessary to avoid creating conflicting contractual obligations for the author between her obligation to her employer and her agreement with a publisher.

Since the Harvard University Faculty of Arts and Sciences adopted the first open-access policy of this type in February 2008, the language and effect of these documents has become standardized and widely understood.[23] The heart of such policies is a perpetual, irrevocable license to the

---

23. The Harvard policies (there have been eight, adopted by eight of the nine Harvard faculties) are available at https://osc.hul.harvard.edu/policies. The Offices of Scholar Communications at Harvard has also offered a very helpful guide to the specific decisions and adaptations that might be made to policy language in a guide found at https://osc.hul.harvard.edu/modelpolicy.

institution for open-access deposit, which can nonetheless be waived by the faculty author. The language of these policies has been refined over the years since then as other institutional faculties have enacted similar licenses, and sometimes changes are made to accommodate local needs and concerns of specific faculties. By 2011 there were enough institutions with some form of OA policy or mandate to form an organization to help members with the implementation of an open-access policy and to encourage others to adopt one. That group, called the Coalition of Open Access Policy Institutions (COAPI), has now grown to include fifty-six colleges, universities, and research centers in North America.[24] In 2012, the United Nations Education, Scientific and Cultural Organization (UNSECO) published a set of *Policy Guidelines for the Development and Promotion of Open Access* (Swan 2012). That document demonstrates the widespread interest in open access in general and institutional policies specifically and will be very useful as more institutional faculties consider adopting such policies.

Different institutions have approached the implementation of these faculty-adopted open-access policies in different ways. Some have largely relied on individual faculty authors to submit their works to the local repository. But since these policies give the institutions the legal right to archive on behalf of the authors, many institutions have taken a more proactive approach and mediated the process of collecting faculty author articles for their repositories. This often involves a discovery system to keep track of new faculty publications, an investigation into publisher policies, and either direct upload of the articles licensed under the policy or a request to the author to supply the final author's manuscript (or "post-print") when the policies of the journal in which the article was published allow archiving of only that version. Although the licenses created by these policies predate any transfer of copyright to a publisher, most institutions have elected, at least so far, not to assert their prior right to archive articles where doing so would place the faculty author in the

---

24. For up-to-date numbers, see the COAPI website at www.sparc.arl.org/COAPI.

difficult position of arguably having licensed the copyright in his or her work in incompatible ways.

The potential for this kind of difficult situation could be greatly reduced if more publishers adopted policies that both protected their own interests and respected the wishes of the authors and copyright holders from whom they obtain the content they publish. A small percentage of publishers now allow self-archiving even of the final published version of an article, either immediately or after a short embargo. As noted above, there is no evidence that such policies harm subscription sales. Other publishers allow authors to archive only the final submitted manuscript in order to preserve their own exclusivity as the source for the "version of record." This is probably the most common stipulation today in publication contracts, and for that reason most faculty-adopted open-access policies grant the license to the institution for deposit specifically of that version.

Unfortunately, at least one major publisher has decided to directly attack the growing tendency for faculty authors to impose a license for deposit in an institutional repository on themselves. As of this writing, the standard copyright transfer agreement used by Elsevier gives back to the author of a published article the right to self-archive unless that author works for an institution that has an open-access policy.[25] This "you may if you do not have to, but you cannot if you must" agreement puts faculty authors in a very difficult position and is a clear attempt to influence the internal campus policies of colleges and universities considering an open-access policy. While the universities that have adopted these policies to date have endeavored to respect the agreements that authors subsequently sign with publishers, this particular publisher has not shown authors the same respect. This clause in an author agreement is really a significant threat to the academic freedom of faculties to adopt policies on their own campuses that they believe

25. There is an explanation of this policy on the Elsevier guide for authors at www. elsevier.com/journal-authors/author-rights-and-responsibilities.

are in the best interests of scholarship, research, and teaching. If it is enforced by Elsevier, it will put institutions in the awkward position of having to decide at what point to assert their prior rights (the license created by policy or even work made for hire rights) over a faculty-authored article.

Green Open Access—Self-Archiving after Traditional Publication

Advantages

- Open to all readers.
- Institutional identification.
- Journal branding and impact factor from original publisher maintained on article-by-article basis.
- Peer review managed by (original) publisher staff.
- Easily searchable (by Google, etc.).
- May be able to associate media and data with self-archived version.

Disadvantages

- Complex licensing with traditional publishers (author must retain rights to self-archive either through publication contract or via an institutionally mandated license).
- Resistance from some publishers.
- May be version discrepancies, depending on license with publisher.
- Potential difficulties consolidating dispersed citation metrics.
- Interface for repository versions often more sparse.
- Reuse rights for archived version often unclear to users.

Direct Web Publication

The final method of disseminating research and achieving maximum access to one's work is to publish that work directly to the Internet without any publishing intermediary. Although this method lacks the "brand name" of a traditional journal and does not usually involve prepublication peer review, it is nonetheless increasing in popularity. One of the advantages of writing directly for the Web is, obviously, that such distribution of scholarship is more informal and more immediate. One can get one's thoughts to a large number of people very quickly and receive responses, comments, and reviews from many more people almost instantaneously. Perhaps for this reason, and also perhaps because the other forms of open access are less well-developed in these discipline groups, many of the most prominent experiments in direct Internet scholarship are from scholars in the humanities and social sciences.

When scholarship is published directly to the Internet without intermediary, it relies on open, post-distribution review, rather than the traditional anonymous peer review. Commentators are not selected in advance, although group blogs, for example, often involve a group of scholars commenting on each other's work. And the comments are not private, of course. If a blog is open to comments, anyone can say anything and, depending on the degree of moderation, anyone can see these comments. This involves a certain risk and requires a willingness to expose disagreement and even correct flaws in public. The upside, however, is that many more voices can be involved, resulting, one hopes, in scholarship that is more comprehensive and inclusive in its focus.

We will look briefly at three types of open Web distribution of scholarship—overlay journals, scholarly blogs and discourse spaces, and digital scholarship projects. In one sense, the overlay journal is not strictly a form of direct Web distribution since it does rely on a type of editorial mediation. But because it shares with these other types of dissemination a reliance on post-distribution review, it is included in this category.

The phrase *overlay journal* refers to a website that organizes and links to selected content on a topic that is openly available elsewhere on the

Web. So the editors of an overlay journal would search the Web for open-access content on a specific topic, then decide what is the best material on that topic to include in an "issue" of their journal. The issue would consist of a series of links, often with an explanation of what the linked material is and why it was included in that particular issue of the overlay journal. In this way the journal truly is an editorial "overlay" on top of accessible Web content. The content selected may have been published elsewhere and made available through either gold OA or self-archiving so that the overlay is providing a second, post-publication level of peer review in addition to that which was done before the initial publication, or it may be material that has been uploaded to a website without any prior peer review. In both cases, the overlay provides an independent validation of these articles that are already openly accessible. Overlay journals add value to open-access scholarship by providing a kind of "branding," by grouping disparate materials together to address a specific topic, and by adding metadata and editorial comment that turns the collection into a unified whole. The *Lund Medical Faculty Monthly*, from Lund University in Sweden, is an example of this kind of Web publication.[26]

Probably the most common form of scholarship that takes place directly online and without access barriers is the scholarly blog. A large and increasing number of scholars are putting ideas and earlier versions of their work up on blogs and inviting comment. In many cases a group of scholars will collaborate on a blog, creating an interdisciplinary discourse space that simply cannot happen in the analog world. The website for HASTAC (www.hastac.org), the Humanities, Arts, Science, and Technology Alliance and Collaboratory, is such a discourse space, hosting blogs, news and event announcements, discussions of pedagogy, "threaded" conversations on specific topics, and Twitter feeds. Its influence, especially in the area of digital humanities, is evidenced by the

---

26. The *Lund Medical Faculty Monthly* can be read at http://www.lmfm.med.lu.se. Note that this example does not merely link to the previously available content but stores copies of the articles on the Lund medical faculty's own servers and provides pointers to the original sources.

number of scholars who participate and the success of the collaboratory in attracting grant support.

Despite scorn from a few skeptics, scholarly blogs are having a significant impact within their fields. One area where this is especially true is legal scholarship. Perhaps because of the unusual structure of legal scholarship, where most of the journals are student-edited law reviews, legal scholars have always been comfortable with more informal forms of critique for their work. So the legal blog is simply a more public form of the collaborative and casual peer review that has long prevailed in the field. Among legal blogs, *The Volokh Conspiracy* (www.washingtonpost.com/news/volokh-conspiracy) and *Balkinization* (http://balkin.blogspot.com) are two that have a significant impact, many contributors, and large followings. Both blogs serve as the first forum for many new scholarly ideas and articles, and both are followed by the press looking for new developments.[27]

Blogs are having an impact even in fields that traditionally depend on more formal types of scholarly publishing. In anthropology, the blog *Savage Minds* (http://savageminds.org) has a roster of ten full-time contributors and many more occasional authors who share their thoughts on significant topics, their latest research interests, and ideas for future publications. The conversation is lively and provides a critique of forthcoming work that involves more scholars from the field, broadly defined, than could ever take part in the double-blind process common to traditional journals. Finally, some scholarly blogs defy disciplinary definition entirely. The blog *Crooked Timber* (http://crookedtimber.org), which takes its name from the famous quote from Immanuel Kant that "out of the crooked timber of humanity no straight thing was ever made," has a group of sixteen current authors that includes philosophers, literary and classical scholars, sociologists, and an economist ("Crooked Timber" 2014). It is broadly focused on political philosophy but is the

27. Both of these blogs are named after their founders, Eugene Volokh from UCLA School of Law and Jack Balkin of Yale Law School, but both have become group blogs on which the dialogue between participants is often the most creative aspect.

site of conversations, many of which draw dozens and even hundreds of responses, about a wide range of current and scholarly topics. All of these blogs illustrate two things. First, many scholars now see blogging as a legitimate and even rewarding way to develop both their scholarship and their scholarly reputations. Second, the immediacy of online discussion among scholars has become an important and creative opportunity for scholarship.

Our third example of online scholarship is probably the most obvious, but in many ways it is also the most hidden. Over the past ten years, many scholars have begun to do legitimate scholarly work that simply cannot be published in any traditional format because it was "born digital." The digital environment offers a tremendous opportunity to work on old problems in a new way and to explore questions that simply could not be addressed in analog scholarship. Digitized collections of texts, for example, can provide new insights into how individual authors worked throughout their careers by using "text mining" and structural comparisons and can also facilitate such studies across the oeuvres of many authors. The site called *Romantic Circles* (www.rc.umd.edu) is an example of this kind of text-based digital project. Data visualizations and online mapping offer another set of new ways to understand scientific or sociological phenomena; one remarkable example is the database called Voyages chronicling the transatlantic slave trade (www.slavevoyages.org/tast/index.faces), which conglomerates a great deal of diverse data to provide maps of slave trade routes, analysis of African names derived from lists of liberated slaves, and data estimates of the size of the ignoble trade in human beings.

In addition to these relatively specific projects in digital scholarship, the online, digitally diverse journal *Vectors* offers an opportunity to "publish" all kinds of digital scholarly works that broadly group around the theme of the impact of technology on daily life. But to say that is to undervalue the innovation found in *Vectors*, which combines all sorts of different digital scholarship on a variety of topics into an online forum that "is realized in multimedia, melding form and content to enact a second-order examination of the mediation of everyday life" ("About *Vectors*" 2014). Among the projects that are included in the "pages" of *Vectors* is a remarkable meditation on the impact of Hurricane Katrina on New Orleans, called "Blue Velvet: Re-dressing New Orleans in Katrina's Wake" (Goldberg and Hristova 2014) that illustrates the possibilities of digital scholarship and the impossibility of accomplishing the same kind of insight in analog publications.

Digital scholarship projects usually cannot be subjected to peer review in the same way that traditional journal articles have been, although *Vectors* is an exception to this general principle. Many of these projects grow out of an individual's scholarly imagination, or a collaboration between several colleagues, and take shape on the Web with little intermediation. Yet they often represent a significant investment of intellectual capital and an important contribution to a field or topic of study. Thus they pose a challenge for the traditional promotion and tenure process, which has traditionally relied on the name of the journal in which an article was published and the names on editorial board that oversees that journal to form an estimate of the quality and impact of a scholar and her work. For those working on born-digital projects, these traditional structures for evaluation are absent. The challenge for university promotion and tenure processes is to find ways to account for and assess these kinds of creative scholarly projects. This challenge will surely grow in the coming years. Conversely, many scholars will continue to rely on traditional forms of publication and even develop analog articles out of digital projects for much longer than they would if all factors were even in order to have the traditional stamp of approval that a "name-brand" journal article provides.

Direct Web Distribution—
Blogs and Web-Based Discourse Spaces

Advantages

- May be only option for dissemination of some types of digital scholarship.
- Usually open to all (creator has option to commercialize).
- Opportunity to tailor interface to suit creator's vision.
- Creator retains copyright and can license reuse as desired.
- No limits, other than technical, on media formats and data associated with scholarly work.
- Searchable, but only if good metadata is associated.
- Available immediately upon creation.

Disadvantages

- Self-managed peer review.
- Institution and readers may not know how to evaluate.
- No brand other than personal reputation.
- May need to create metadata in order to optimize usability.
- Need to continue to preserve and update; possibility that work will be ephemeral.
- Usage analytics will be more variable and usually more basic (e.g., Google Analytics).

CONCLUSION

As in the time of Galileo, the landscape for disseminating scholarship in the twenty-first century is uncertain and confusing. All of the familiar outlets that have served scholars for the past three centuries are still with us, but the digital environment also offers an array of new opportunities, including the chance to reach previously inaccessible and even unimaginable readers for scholarly work. The older and newer models for scholarly publication often conflict, especially over how the copyright, which always resides first with the author, can best be managed. For those who select the more traditional modes of publication, the publication contract is the key to copyright management, and the ability to also take advantage of digital dissemination depends, in large measure, on the provisions that that contractual agreement contains or are added in the negotiation process. For online dissemination, whether it is undertaken as an adjunct to traditional publication, as in green open access, or as the sole method by which the scholarship in question will reach its audience, as in gold open access or direct Web distribution, another issue arises. When readers encounter a work on the Web, they should realize that it is likely to be protected by copyright, and they will rightly wonder what they may do with the article or book they have found. They can surely read it on their screen, but can they print it out? May they distribute it further, either by posting it to some online forum or by handing out printed copies to, for example, a classroom of students? The online environment raises these questions, which have always been important regarding copyrighted works, in a new and urgent way. Thus the question of licensing becomes more important than ever, since it is by licenses that these and many other questions regarding the use of protected works must be answered. In our next chapter, we will examine the issue of licenses, as well as one other way in which use can be controlled, technological protection measures, more closely.

Beyond Copyright: Licensing and Technological Protection Measures

IN *HOLLYWOOD'S* *Copyright Wars: From Edison to the Internet*, media scholar Peter Decherney (2012) details the continuous and continuing conflict over copyright that the ever-developing technologies of film and video have generated. The interesting point is that those conflicts have seldom actually been resolved in the federal courts. Instead, the film industries have usually found extralegal means, or at least means that are outside the system of federal copyright protection, to ultimately resolve their problems.

Early in their history, for example, each movie studio used different film formats, varying the number and pattern of sprocket holes in order to create a vertically integrated market. This early form of technological protection measure, however, proved to actually encourage piracy since rivals simply copied other studios' entire films onto their own proprietary formats. After several lawsuits, the studios eventually formed cooperative agreements to license their films to one another rather than continuing to engage in a war no one could win. In a similar way, authors who resented the uncompensated use of their ideas first tried copyright litigation to protect the market for film adaptations. When they were largely defeated by the idea/expression dichotomy in copyright law, they began to form organizations that would draft model licenses. It ultimately became the easier and less expensive industry standard to use these license agreements to avoid the expense and delay caused by copyright litigation.[1]

In these examples, we see that copyright has always seemed too porous, with all of its limitations and exceptions, for some rights holders. Whenever this is the case, one of two routes, which are sometimes referred to together as "paracopyright," is used to achieve greater protection. One option is to rely on licensing agreements, which are contracts enforced under state laws that are far more adaptable than a federal statute like copyright. Indeed, licenses are a way in which copyright holders can leverage their rights to get either greater *or lesser* protection, depending on their perceived needs. We will examine this type of "private" legal protection for copyrights in the first part of this chapter.

The other form of "paracopyright," which will be discussed in the latter part of this chapter, is technological protection measures. As technologies have developed, all kinds of measures to prevent unauthorized access and copying have been utilized by rights holders and their agents. From different-sized sprocket holes to the complex encryption that protects commercial films distributed on DVD or as online streams, these technological barriers are a sort of last resort for rights holders who feel that copyright does not protect them completely enough or when, as in the digital age, they fear that copyright will simply be ignored.

In the digital age, these technological protection measures (TPMs), which are also sometimes referred to as DRM or "digital rights management," have become especially important to rights holders and often extremely obnoxious to consumers. In 1998, as part of the Digital Millennium Copyright Act, Congress made the "circumvention" of technologi-

---

1. Decherney 2012. On writers' efforts to protect the ideas in their works, see pages 90–101; regarding projection technology and the "patent trust" see pages 11–36.

cal protection measures an act punishable by the same civil and criminal penalties as copyright infringement. Since then, there have been repeated conflicts over the exceptions to these anti-circumvention rules and how far they should extend to allow scholars and consumers to copy protected works without authorization. We will discuss this ongoing debate later on.

LICENSING

Licensing in General

A license is also a contract, but it works differently from an assignment or transfer of copyright. With a license, a rights holder gives to another permission to exercise all or part of the right that he or she holds, but does not surrender that right. As an example, suppose I give permission to my nephew to use my car. I do not lose ownership of my car by doing so; I simply allow him to use the car without the risk of being arrested for auto theft. I have the right to exclusive use of the car I own, but I can forego that exclusivity by licensing the right to another. My license may be exclusive, in which I promise my nephew that only he will use the car (i.e., exercise the right that I am licensing) for some period of time. Or I can give him a non-exclusive license, in which I allow him to use the car but retain the option of allowing others to use it as well, although the physical nature of the car makes it impossible for two licensees to use it at the same time, which is not true of two non-exclusive licensees of intellectual property. Licenses to exercise all or some of the rights under copyright can likewise be exclusive or non-exclusive; an exclusive license must be in writing.

Publication under License

While most publication contracts are transfers of copyright, some publishers do use licenses instead. In all of these cases, the author (now referred to as the licensor) retains the copyright, subject to the conditions in the license. When a publisher must depend on subscriptions to support its publication, it is most common to use an exclusive license, at least among the minority that use a license at all.

Perhaps the best-known publisher that uses an exclusive license rather than a transfer of copyright is Nature Publishing Group (NPG), which publishes the prestigious journal *Nature,* as well as several other scientific journals. NPG takes an exclusive license to publish from its authors, who retain the copyright in their articles. Those authors also retain the right to "reuse their papers in their future printed work without first requiring permission from the publisher of the journal."[2] Because this license is exclusive, it is nearly as limiting for the author as a transfer would be, but it is worthwhile to notice the difference. Since the license is to publish, which presumably implicates the rights of reproduction and distribution, authors retain control over the other rights in the copyright bundle, specifically public performance, public display, and the preparation of derivative works. Public performance presumably means that an author could read her paper at a scholarly conference without gaining permission, and the derivative works right would give the author the right, for example, to create a visualization of findings in the article for her website without seeking permission. Other activities that do implicate the licensed rights of reproduction and distribution require the author to get permission from NPG, which is now the exclusive licensee of those rights; that is why reprinting in future works must be specifically allowed. Likewise, NPG grants back to licensors a specific and limited right to self-archive their articles; they are permitted to do so after a period of six months has elapsed from first publication and may do so only in PubMed Central, the NIH-mandated repository; in an institutional repository; or on a personal web page.

---

2. See the full description of NPG's licensing and authors' rights policy at NPG 2012.

Non-exclusive licenses for publication are generally found only for journals that are openly accessible without a subscription fee. Because these open-access publishers do not need exclusivity to protect a revenue stream, they generally ask only for a non-exclusive license to reproduce and distribute an article in their journal. In those cases, the author retains the copyright and the ability to exercise any of the rights that are part of copyright, as well as to permit others to exercise any of those rights.

Software Licenses and Terms of Use

The real explosion of licenses in both personal and academic life has come because of the licenses associated with software and application downloads, as well as the trend toward licensing content from online services rather than buying it outright. Today most people are aware that when they sign up to use iTunes or Facebook or Kindle, they are agreeing to a license that governs how they may use the online service and even the content that they "purchase" through that service. And some are even aware that those licenses may also give the online vendor certain rights in the content that the users themselves upload to a service like Facebook. In late 2012, there was a brief controversy over an announcement from the photo-sharing service Instagram that its new license with users would give it the right to sell photos uploaded by those users, even for commercial purposes. The outcry that ensued caused Instagram to back down,[3] but the incident is only the latest reminder that online licenses can often work two ways; they can control how purchasers may use the product and give rights in the intellectual property created by those users to the company that runs the service. Although most people will ruefully admit that they have never read one of these online documents (the one for Apple's iTunes prints to over thirty pages), these kinds of

---

3. For one of many online news reports about this incident, see McCullagh and Tam 2012.

controversies demonstrate how much of our online lives can now be controlled by licenses.

The appeal of a licensing transaction over a direct sale for vendors of intellectual property should be fairly obvious; it rests in the ability to control "downstream" uses of the IP. The desire for such control occasionally manifested itself even before digital content became so ubiquitous. In the early 2000s, the Maryland State Bar Association, for example, marketed its *Lawyers' Manual* in shrink-wrap with a license that attempted to forbid purchasers from loaning the book to anyone. Thus it hoped to sell a copy of this important directory to every Maryland attorney rather than having all of the lawyers in a large firm use just one or two copies. In a law review article, Professor Elizabeth Winston (2006, 2) recounts this incident and describes the benefits that vendors hope to gain by licensing IP instead of selling it. Rather than being subject to the well-developed restrictions on consumer sales in general, and specific IP doctrines like the doctrine of first sale (which is what the Maryland Bar Association was trying to avoid), such licensing transactions are governed entirely by the terms negotiated between the parties. Such "privately legislated" rules, to use Winston's term, offer a great deal more flexibility, including the possibility of avoiding such publicly legislated doctrines as first sale and fair use. In short, they can allow the vendor to control what the licensee (who often thinks of herself as a purchaser rather than a licensee) can do with the IP after the transaction is complete—how she can use it and make it available to others.

Because such downstream uses are so much more threatening in the digital environment, where the click of a mouse can send a work of IP to millions of others in essentially perfect copies, this control offered by licenses is exponentially more important to vendors of intellectual property in the digital age, and licenses of all sorts have proliferated. On an almost daily basis, ordinary consumers are asked to click on I Agree before obtaining access to some online product or service. And in spite of the reference above to negotiation between the license parties, most of these licenses are presented as "take it or leave it" propositions. Consumers must either accept the terms of the license as presented or forgo the product; no opportunity to negotiate exists. Such licenses are an example of what is called a "contract of adhesions" because the only choice the licensee has is to adhere (or not) to the terms. Before the digital age, courts looked with great suspicion on contracts of adhesion, but their ubiquity and efficiency in the digital environment has radically altered that approach. Although there is not unanimity among courts on this topic, as a general rule a "click-through" contract that requires an affirmative act of acceptance and that makes the terms relatively easy to see if one wants to do so will be enforceable. If, on the other hand, the terms of the license are available but not obvious and no mouse click is necessary to accept those terms, courts may be less willing to enforce the terms.

An interesting case study in digital licensing is presented by e-readers and the e-books that can be bought for them. When one buys a book for a Kindle or Nook e-reader, that "purchase" is clearly a licensing transaction. The license restricts the use of the e-book to personal use, often forbids lending of the digital file, and limits the number of devices onto which the e-book may be downloaded. But the device itself is sold to the consumer and is presumably governed by the publicly legislated rules that govern such sales of tangible property, including those that favor the unrestricted right to lend, sell, or rent one's own property at will. So the odd situation is presented in which it is clear that an e-book licensee may not lend the books she has licensed but appears to be able to lend the device on which those books are legally downloaded. Library programs that lend e-readers full of popular content are depending on this distinction, and to my knowledge no vendor of the devices and content has yet challenged the practice. But it is still an anomalous and unsettled situation created by the unique properties of digital content and the licenses that govern that content.

Individual versus Enterprise-wide Licensing in Academia

As was mentioned when we discussed licenses as "private legislation" above, a license, like any other contract, is binding only on those who are a party to it. Because of this fact and the complex interplay between these private-law licenses and the public law that generally governs IP and binds all citizens, it is often important to know exactly who the parties to an intellectual property license are. To illustrate by continuing the case study regarding a Kindle e-reader, suppose I do decide to lend my e-reader to my friend so that she can read the books I have downloaded. As we have seen, it is unsettled as to whether or not I am allowed to do this based on the licenses to which I have agreed. But my friend is not a party to any of those licenses. There is little doubt, for example, that she would violate neither the terms of any contract nor the public IP laws if she went ahead and read the books on the device I loaned to her. If, however, she made a copy of one of those e-books and loaned it to her sister (assuming that do that was technologically possible, a subject we will get to in a while), she would have infringed (probably) the reproduction and distribution rights in federal copyright law entirely independently of my contractual obligations as the original licensee.

Deciding who is bound by an IP license, and therefore who might be liable for breach of contract if its terms are violated, becomes much more complicated when scholars download software applications, or content while employed by, and often on equipment belonging to, a college or university. The individual who clicks on I Accept is certainly a party to the contract and liable for its breach. But is the institution? That will depend on a determination of whether or not the individual scholar acted as an "agent" for her employer or not. The law of agency is complex, but as a general rule, if the employee was acting within the scope of her employment—if the motivation of the action was to benefit the employer by doing her job effectively—the acceptance of contractual terms will generally bind the institution as well as the individual.[4] So when a teacher downloads a program needed to draw charts that he will use in the classroom, or a scientist downloads specialized statistical software to use in her research, that individual is likely acting within the scope of his or her employment so that the institution would also be considered a party to the license.

Problems in this scenario can come from two different directions—the institution may have rules about who is allowed to accept contracts on its behalf, and the vendor may present its licensing terms in such a way as to provoke an invalid consent.

If an institution has a policy about who may sign contracts on behalf of the institution, it would be conceivable, although unlikely, that the institution could try to avoid obligations under a license accepted by an employee by claiming that the acceptance was outside the scope of the employee's job. Doing this would provoke a fight with the licensor and would also create hard feelings, obviously, between employer and employee. But even though it is unlikely, it is worth noting that it is a possible way for an employer to escape liability under an end-user license agreement (EULA) accepted by an employee and could be a last resort if the terms of such a license were especially repugnant to the institution.

A more realistic set of problems, which have actually begun to arise, at least in the academic library world, comes about when a vendor decides to impose terms for a business product used by multiple people within an institution through an end-user license. For years, universities have

---

4. In this situation, the liability for any breach of the contractual terms would be "joint and several," meaning that both the institution and the individual could be sued, and any damages assessed could be collected from either party. Such collection of damages would not have to be equal or proportional; the plaintiff would be entitled to get the money from whichever source he can. In practice, this usually means that the institution is the focus of any litigation since the institution is better able, usually, to pay damages. For this reason, a university will almost always act to defend a lawsuit brought because an individual in its employ accepted licensing terms while acting within the scope of her employment. The situation in which the institution asserts that the employee was not acting within the scope of her employment and therefore must face the suit alone is rare, but it is not impossible.

negotiated "enterprise-wide" licenses for software packages and online databases that they have purchased. But in the online environment, several vendors of such products have decided that it is too expensive and time-consuming to negotiate individual licenses and have decided, instead, to use a click-through license that must be accepted by the employee who actually logs in to use the database. Since such employees seldom actually have the authority to accept licensing terms on behalf of the institution, these EULAs can be especially problematic. Furthermore, these EULAs often contain terms that the institution would not accept if the vendor had negotiated directly with the customer. Public institutions, for example, are often forbidden by state law from accepting indemnification clauses or submitting to legal jurisdiction in another state, yet the EULAs for several products intended for enterprise-wide use have contained these clauses.[5]

In the past, these kinds of licensing concerns were handled without the need for individual teachers and researchers to be aware of them. In the online environment, however, this has changed dramatically. The situation for software and online information licensing and access has become extremely complex and fraught with difficulties. Almost all scholars encounter and accept such licenses, and it is necessary to be attentive to them and aware of their pitfalls, not only to be a good citizen of the academy, but also to avoid potential liability and disputes with one's employer.

Creative Commons Licensing

We have already discussed Creative Commons licenses in some detail in chapter 4, focusing on how such licenses facilitated the reuse of original

---

5. The library book vendor Yankee Book Peddler announced in late 2012 that it would institute such an EULA but withdrew the plan after the academic library community objected, largely for the reasons explained in the text. The Copyright Clearance Center, on the other hand, has apparently been using a similarly objectionable EULA for several years; see Smith 2012b for more information.

materials by teachers and scholars. In this section, we focus briefly on another aspect of these licenses, their utility for the scholars who want to distribute their own work, as opposed to using the work of others, with a Creative Commons license.

As we explained in the discussion about use, the Creative Commons license allows the creator of a work, or another rights holder, to grant prior permission for others to use that work in a broad spectrum of ways. It also allows the rights holder to select from a predetermined set of conditions that will be imposed on all uses permitted under the license. Thus a creator may allow her work to be reused only as long as the user gives her credit for the original work, makes only a noncommercial use of that original, and shares whatever new work is created by the use under the same license as the original. Such a license would be said to have "Attribution-NonCommercial-ShareAlike" terms. An attribution requirement is a part of almost all Creative Commons licenses.[6] The second term may be set to allow only noncommercial uses; if it is excluded from the license, then uses that meet the other conditions will be permitted whether or not they are commercial in nature. Finally, the third term of most CC licenses addresses the issue of whether or not derivative works are allowed; its values include "no derivative works" or the "ShareAlike" term mentioned above. If neither value is selected, derivative works would be allowed under the license and could be distributed in any way the second creator saw fit.

These licenses hold substantial attraction for academics. As we have noted before, there is actually no attribution requirement in United States copyright law. But attribution—the ability to get credit for one's work—is the lifeblood of the academic rewards system. Since there is generally no significant revenue available to a scholarly author, attribution is often the most valuable aspect of intellectual property since only attribution can support an academic reputation and make the rewards that are avail-

6. The only exception would be the CC 0 license, which is an attempt to waive copyright entirely and dedicate the work to the public domain. See Creative Commons 2014a.

able—promotion, tenure, and influence—possible. Thus the Creative Commons licenses, with their attribution term, offer a way for scholars to leverage their ownership of copyright in a way that protects the most important of academic values, credit for one's work.

The importance of the other terms of a CC license will vary depending on the needs of the scholarly creator. Some authors and creators may be happy to see their work used for purposes of commercial development, for example, while others will want to retain control over such potential uses. When a CC license carries a "NonCommercial" condition, anyone interested in making a commercial use would have to contact the rights holder and negotiate separately regarding that use.[7] And whether or not derivative works will be allowed might depend on the type of material being licensed. Teaching resources, for example, would really be useful only if derivative works are allowed since each instructor making use of such licensed resources will want to adapt them to his or her own teaching style. On the other hand, doctoral dissertations, the authors of which frequently wish to revise them for publication, should probably not be licensed for derivative works since the existence of such derivatives might undermine the authors' future publication plans.[8]

Creative Commons Licenses and Open-Access Journals

It is precisely because of these advantages for scholars and scholarship that many open-access publishers distribute the articles in their gold or hybrid open-access journals with Creative Commons licenses. For

---

7.   The definition of a commercial versus noncommercial use has been subject to some misunderstanding and controversy in regard to the CC licensing schema. The CC did some research on the issue and published a report (Creative Commons 2009) that provides some perspective on the issue but does not wholly resolve the question.

8.   In the Duke University repository for online theses and dissertations, the default license granted by each author is a Creative Commons Attribution-NonCommercial-NoDerivs license. This option was chosen to protect attribution, of course, preserve the authors' rights in regard to commercial exploitation, and prevent derivative works that could impact later publication.

example, the major academic publisher Springer announced in January 2012 that all of its open-access articles, including those in its gold SpringerOpen journals, articles published through its hybrid Open Choice program, and all of the BioMed Central journals, which Springer also owns, would be published with a CC Attribution (CC BY) license (Springer 2012). The same license is used by all of the journals published by the Public Library of Science (PLOS 2014). Although these are prominent examples of open-access journals using CC licenses, many OA journals do not make the reuse situation clear to readers; this is extremely unfortunate since the default assumption in these cases is that all rights are reserved.

As the Springer press release makes clear, a large part of the reason for its change to an attribution-only license was to facilitate commercial uses of published research. Since one of the major emphases of the open-access movement is to speed up research and development for the betterment of society, allowing commercial uses of OA research makes sense. It is seldom the case, after all, that a researcher would have the facilities or the capital to translate his academic research into a product that could be monetized. Nevertheless, it is important for scholars publishing with these open-access journals to understand the terms under which others will be able to use their work. Most often, the assurance of attribution is all that really matters, but in some cases a researcher, especially if she anticipates a patent application, may wish to avoid this kind of license for her publications related to that invention that appear prior to filing the patent application. And there are a few open-access publications that still use a CC attribution, noncommercial license—the *Yale Journal of Biology and Medicine* (http://medicine.yale.edu/yjbm/index.aspx) is one example—that preserves the final decision about permitting a commercial use for the author.[9]

---

9.   For an article that discusses these licensing options for open-access journals, see MacCallum 2007.

The final point to make about the use of Creative Commons licensing with open-access publications is that because of this licensing, authors almost always retain their copyright in the works they have published. Because of its breadth, the CC license granted by the author extends sufficient rights for the journal to publish the work and for users to use the work in all meaningful academic ways while leaving the copyright with the author. Thus the authors grant permission for a pretty wide range of uses of their articles, but they retain the copyright and have the final say over any uses that fall outside the license grant. In this sense, publishing in an open-access journal under a Creative Commons is a tradeoff; it involves granting much broader rights than a journal reader would ordinarily have (although they are rights that usually not only do not harm the authors but probably benefit them) while allowing the authors to retain control over all residual rights.

TECHNOLOGICAL PROTECTION MEASURES

Another way, in addition to licensing, in which owners of copyrighted material attempt to control access and use more securely and efficiently than simply relying on the copyright law is through technological protection measures. Such measures are not really new; the chains that secured books to the shelves in medieval libraries were, after all, a form of technology that "effectively controlled access" to the books.[10] The medieval librarians were protecting books, which were then rare and expensive, from loss. In the digital environment, new technologies have developed to protect books and many other kinds of intellectual property from mass duplication and distribution in near-perfect copies. DVDs are sold with encryption built in, e-books are locked to specific devices, and music files are purchased in a form that controls the number of copies that can be

---

10. This is a paraphrase of the language from section 1201 of the Copyright Act (17 U.S.C. § 1201 (a)) that provides legal security for digital locks. We will discuss that legal security in detail later in the text.

made onto different devices. In this new situation, technological protection measures are often referred to as "digital rights management" or, more informally, as "digital locks." We will use these terms synonymously, as well as the acronyms TPMs and DRM.

The fundamental difficulty with using software routines to encode security into a digital product is that almost as soon as a clever piece of code is created and deployed, another programmer will create a piece of code that will unlock the digital lock created by the first programmer. The case of the DRM system used with DVDs is illustrative. "Content Scrambling System," or CSS, has been used to prevent copying of the content from a DVD for quite a while. But the code to decrypt protected DVDs, called deCSS, began to circulate very soon after the first coded discs were released. It became ubiquitous on the Web, and one could even buy t-shirts that displayed the code needed to unlock a DVD.[11] This "arms race" over digital encryption led to an ironic move on the part of rights holders, especially from the music and motion picture industries. Having deployed TPMs in order to avoid having to rely on the slow and uncertain mechanisms of legal enforcement for copyright, they ultimately turned back to those legal mechanisms to protect the protection systems they were inventing.

In 1998, as part of the Digital Millennium Copyright Act (Pub. L. No. 105-304, 112 Stat. 2860), Congress added a set of provisions to the copyright law to address "circumvention" of technological protection measures—actions that could unlock technological locks or undermine efforts at digital rights management. This new provision of the law makes it illegal, subject to the same penalties as copyright infringement, to circumvent digital locks and technological protection measures. It also prohibits the removal or falsification of copyright management information, as well as the manufacture, importation, or sale of technology the primary purpose of which is the circumvention of TPMs.

---

11. For a brief history of deCSS, see "DeCSS" 2014.

In addition to these basic prohibitions, this new section of the law contains quite a number of exceptions and qualifications to the basic prohibitions. Many of these specify particular activities for the accomplishment of which limited circumvention of TPMs is permitted. These include encryption research, law enforcement activities, and reverse engineering for the purpose of determining interoperability. For scholars, however, the most important parts of this section of exceptions are not these specific exceptions but two provisions that are quite vague and have been subject to much subsequent discussion. One is the so-called "savings clause" (17 U.S.C. § 1201(c)), which explicitly states that nothing in this new section of the law shall affect the limitations and exceptions to copyright, including fair use. The savings clause also states that TPMs and "anti-circumvention" rules should not be used to limit free speech or freedom of the press. And, apparently because Congress felt that even these broad exceptions might not be sufficient to avoid harm that could be done by digital locking, authority is given to the Librarian of Congress to determine, every three years, what "classes of work" should be exempted from the ban on circumvention—that is, situations in which breaking the digital locks should be allowed—because enforcement of the ban in those cases might have an "adverse effect" on permitted, non-infringing use of copyrighted materials. It is this last provision that has been a source of both relief and frustration to scholars.

In regard to the exception allowing circumvention of TPMs for purposes of free speech or fair use, the courts have been quite active. When dealing with deCSS, discussed above, courts ordered a complete ban on dissemination of the simple code that can decrypt a commercial DVD, ordering the authors of that code to accomplish its complete removal from the Internet, a task even more arduous than the Herculean effort to cleanse the Augean stables![12] There has been considerable discussion about whether or not distribution of the code on t-shirts, which are, of

---

12. The important case is Universal City Studios v. Corley, 273 F.3d 429 (2d Cir. 2001). The case began in the Southern District of New York against a different defendant named Reimerdes and also spun off several additional lawsuits.

course, non-executable, should be included in this ban or is encompassed by the protection for free speech (see Crasson 2004). Fair use and the anti-circumvention rules have had an equally checkered history. In one oft-cited case, a judge held that a defendant could not claim that the underlying purpose for which he circumvented TPMs was fair use because he could have had access to the material in question another way, such a filming the output of a DVD on a television screen using an analog video recording camera. In this case the judge basically found that the savings clause regarding fair use was irrelevant because TPMs control access, and fair use does not guarantee any specific mode of access to a work (see Universal City Studios v. Reimerdes, 82 F. Supp. 2d 211 (SDNY 2000)). Later cases have found more scope for fair use, especially when DRM protections are clearly being used to suppress legitimate competition in the marketplace, but it is still true that reliance on fair use as a justification for circumventing TPMs would be a risky decision in the current legal environment.

For academics, the place where TPMs have had the most immediate impact is when using films on DVD for teaching. Because it is hard to "cue up" a specific spot on a DVD, instructors often need to copy clips from one disc onto another so that specific portions of a work can be played and compared to other clips from other films. Doing this would violate the protection accorded to TPMs, and this was the situation that caught the attention of the Library of Congress in 2006 and prompted the only explicit exemption for scholars to the anti-circumvention rules.[13]

The first such exemption, declared by the Librarian of Congress in 2006, was really designed to address exactly the situation just outlined, and it was tailored very narrowly. In a sense the history of that exemption is a case study in the power of effective storytelling. When the Library announced its second round of rulemaking, pursuant to the authority it was given in the DMCA, it held hearings in order to make its determination about "classes of works" that should be exempted from the prohibi-

---

13. Smith 2006 is a general discussion of the role of DRM in academia.

tion on breaking digital locks. At one of those hearings, a film studies professor testified about the difficulties he had presenting and comparing clips from different films in order to illustrate filmmaking techniques to his students. In response, the Library of Congress fashioned a narrow exemption to solve that specific problem—it applied only to professors of film and media studies and allowed circumvention only for the purpose of compiling clips from DVDs for the purpose of classroom teaching.

In its next two rounds of making exemptions, the Library of Congress has broadened this rule at the persistent request of higher education groups. The 2009 version (which was not announced until July 2010) of the exemption allowed all faculty in higher education (but not at the K–12 level) to circumvent for teaching purposes, as well as to create noncommercial videos that incorporate short clips from encrypted films. It applied, however, only to decrypting DVDs that were protected by CSS, not to other forms of digital materials that might be used in teaching, like video games.[14]

The exemption for education that currently exists is best understood as a further growth and extension of this history, but it is also a testament, in its complexity and convoluted rules, to the compromises that had to made with rights holders, who are very afraid of online distribution of unencrypted versions of their products. Briefly, the rule declared in October 2012 allows circumvention of technological protection measures that control access to two kinds of works—DVDs that are encrypted with CSS, and motion pictures that are distributed through online services, regardless of the type of TPM employed. For these two classes of works, circumvention is allowed when it is reasonably necessary (i.e., other forms of access will not be sufficient for the purpose) in order to use short portions of a film, and short portions only, for the purpose of criticism and comment in other noncommercial videos and documentary films, and for teaching that requires "close analysis." This last permission now includes teachers at the K–12 level, as well as both students and faculty at

---

14. Smith 2010 is a more comprehensive discussion of this exemption.

the university level. It is also worth noting that another exemption now exists that permits circumvention of TPMs on the same classes of work when that circumvention is necessary for research in to how to create playback devices that will be accessible for persons with visual or auditory disabilities. That exemption specifies, however, that the playback device itself may not rely on circumvention.[15]

Because this rulemaking occurs every three years, and because the exemptions are so complicated and involve such finely negotiated distinctions, it is especially important that scholars who believe they need to rely on circumventing a technological protection measure be aware of the current state of the exemptions. It may also be necessary to seek the advice of campus attorneys if there is any doubt about the application of one of the exemptions declared by the Library of Congress.

TPMs and the Future

Not so long ago, it would have been possible to pronounce on the declining relevance of DRM and technological protection measures. The music industry, which really led the way with online distribution for digital content, began to respond to consumer pressure and to remove TPMs from the files that it sold to individuals. Thus it has become easier to move one's music collection from device to device, which is especially important as more and more people use their cell phones for listening to music. But in other areas, the impact of TPMs is still being felt. Electronic books are one example, where digital books are tied to specific devices and, often, lending of those books is prohibited. In 2011, for example, there was considerable controversy over a proposal from one publisher to distribute e-books for libraries with a special form of digital rights management software that would destroy the file after it had been lent a certain number of times, pegged to an alleged average number of loans

---

15. The full text of the 2012 exemptions is found in the Federal Register 77, no. 208 (October 26, 2012): 65260–65279. That portion of the *Federal Register* is also available at the Library of Congress website at www.copyright.gov/fedreg/2012/77fr65260.pdf.

that a print volume in a library is subject to. This was an attempt to use DRM to simulate the conditions of the analog world and thus avoid the persistent threat that content producers feel from the digital environment. Indeed, there are several e-book publishers that simply will not sell their products to libraries at all (see Minzesheimer 2011). The advent of film-streaming services has created another aspect of the consumer entertainment industry where TPMs are still in heavy use, as evidenced by the new language regarding them in the 2012 Library of Congress exemption. And even as some music producers have stopped using DRM software, libraries have become concerned that licensing terms are now used for much digital music sold online, some of which is not available in any other form, which prevent any form of lending and make it impossible for libraries to acquire those pieces.[16]

CONCLUSION

As complex as copyright law is, the use of licenses and TPMs for the distribution of digital content makes the landscape even more confusing and harder to navigate. Yet we should not leave this topic without observing that there are instances in which scholars themselves need these tools for going beyond the protections of copyright. In chapter 4, we discussed the TEACH Act, which allows digital transmission of certain copyrighted performances for teaching purposes, and one of the requirements of the TEACH Act is that the materials be protected from capture and redistribution by "reasonable technical measures." So there are instances where a scholar must use TPMs in order to take advantage of other benefits provided by the law.

In other cases, it may be necessary to control access to certain materials during the course of ongoing research to prevent premature distribu-

---

16. Houghton 2010 is an interesting discussion of the problems of digital music in libraries.

tion. For example, a lab that is collecting and analyzing data may want scholars from distant campuses to participate in that effort, but still want to protect the data prior to full publication. In those cases, some kind of authenticated access, a form of technological protection, is usually called for. Likewise, it is common to provide no access, or campus-only access, to some online dissertations in order to provide authors with a window of exclusivity in which to prepare for more formal publication. Finally, the growth of projects categorized as "digital humanities" has given rise to several efforts at technological protection and new uses for licensing. If "text mining" is involved, for example, restricted access to the texts themselves is probably necessary to conform with the copyright law (assuming the texts to be not public domain) even though the resultant analysis may be distributed widely. Where visualizations are involved, TPMs may be used to control who can contribute to the scholarly product, and even after public release a license, such as the CC "no-derivatives," may be needed to protect the scholarly integrity of the product.

For all of these reasons, both the potential of licensing and TPMs to inhibit scholarship and their growing importance to scholars, it is necessary to be familiar with the complex world of licensing and with the ever-changing landscape of technological protection measures. While these developments complicate an already messy environment for scholarship, they are an unavoidable part of the world in which scholarship must be undertaken today.

Text Mining—A Licensing Quandary

One of the exciting new opportunities that the digital environment for scholarship offers is the prospect of running various kinds of computational analysis of a wide variety of new "data," including large collections of textual material. Of course, there is no copyright problem at all with an analysis run across a large body of public domain literature, as Franco Moretti (2005) does in *Maps, Graphs, Trees*. But what if the data one wants to analyze is itself protected by copyright or subject to licensing terms? In that situation, there are several strands that must be untangled.

The first point to make is that the output of such an analysis—the numerical or graphical results of the computational process—is almost certainly a fair use and therefore does not need permission from the copyright owner. This kind of analysis, which does not "consume" the copyright works in any traditional or expected way, seems like a classic transformative fair use.

In a 2014 revision to its copyright law, the United Kingdom has adopted a provision that specific authorizes text mining without permission from a rights holder in the underlying data corpus (see Intellectual Property Office 2014).

To do such an analysis, however, usually requires that a large corpus of works be downloaded in order to run the program. This download, if its purpose is only to perform a computational analysis so that the texts themselves will not be released or distributed in any way, may well itself be fair use. Access to this kind of text corpus, however, is often restricted by licensing terms, and it is not uncommon that the license might forbid large-scale or systematic downloads, even if such downloads would be fair use under the copyright law. These licensing terms are usually considered to "trump" fair use in such situations.

The lesson to learn from this situation is to be very careful about licensing terms that would inhibit the exploitation of new, and presumptively legal, opportunities like text mining. In recent years, some database producers have begun to offer licensing terms designed to "facilitate" text mining on the corpus of the databases they sell. But these license terms routinely restrict the kind of access and computations that are available, generally by allowing only their own proprietary API to be used. Sometimes the license terms also require detailed disclosure of the type of research in advance and even place limits on how the research "output" can be disseminated. Given the legal situation described above, such license terms actually seem more harmful than helpful, in spite of the stated purpose of making text mining possible. It is worth noting that a Creative Commons license is an excellent way to offer textual material to the public so that text mining can genuinely be facilitated.

Intellectual Property in a World without Borders

THROUGHOUT THIS book we have discussed intellectual property in the context of the law of the United States and in light of the dramatic changes wrought by the advent of digital communications and the Internet. But until now we have ignored one obvious point. The Internet largely disregards the boundaries established by nations as the extent of their sovereignty and the reach of their laws. Digital communications cross international borders without stopping at customs or immigration checkpoints. So how do national laws, including the US law that we have discussed throughout this work, apply to the transnational Internet?

It is probably necessary to state a basic principle at the beginning of this part of our discussion, which has been assumed up till now—national laws, including the law of copyright, do apply to the Internet even though that application can create some previously unanticipated problems.[1] Not

---

1. In *Who Controls the Internet? Illusions of a Borderless World,* Jack Goldsmith and Tim Wu (2006) discuss the belief of some of its founders that the Internet would be a place governed by shared norms rather than national laws and demonstrate that that belief has not been borne out as nations have found ways to apply their national laws to Internet activities.

only in the area of copyright, but in such diverse fields of law as unfair trade, defamation, and antidiscrimination, individual nations do apply their own legal regimes to communications that take place online. In regard to copyright, most nations view their laws as technology-neutral, meaning that the same basic rights and exceptions that apply in the analog world, where they were designed primarily to deal with printed texts, are expected to apply to the digital environment as well. Different nations have made selected changes to their national laws to address specific online issues, but in general we apply the same copyright law to the Internet as we do in the analog world under this basic assumption of technological neutrality.

BOUNDED JURISDICTIONS IN AN UNBOUNDED ENVIRONMENT

The principle of technological neutrality, however, does not address an even more fundamental question—which nation's laws will apply to any given dispute, and which nation's courts will be called upon to resolve that dispute? We will discuss the international treaties that attempt to harmonize copyright laws across borders in a moment, but some comments about these jurisdictional issues seem required first.

Most legal disputes begin when someone files a lawsuit. It is the plaintiff, the person or entity that makes the initial complaint, who decides in the first instance where to file the lawsuit, usually in the court system most convenient to where the plaintiff lives or does business. But once a lawsuit is filed, the court to which it has been directed must decide if it is the correct "venue" for the lawsuit. When the case involves an alleged wrong, such as copyright infringement, that has occurred online, courts generally apply one of two ways to determine if they should hear a case or direct it to some other jurisdiction.

The simple way to decide about jurisdiction over an Internet case is the "server rule." Several courts have embraced this principle, which simply says that the best courts to handle a dispute over some online communication are the courts in the area where the servers that host or hosted the disputed communication are located. The appeal of the server rule is that it provides a well-defined and objective criterion to determine the appropriate jurisdiction. The obvious difficulty with it, however, is that the Internet seldom offers us such well-defined boundaries. Websites and other Internet communications may well be "mirrored" on multiple servers so that a rule based on server location does not offer a simple solution. And in the age of "cloud" computing, the location of the servers in question may point us to a court that would actually have no logical interest in hearing the case in question.

Imagine, for example, a claim that a website written by a resident of California has defamed a resident of Ireland. The Irish victim may want to file her lawsuit in Dublin, while the Californian would prefer to defend against it in the California courts. If a court decided to apply the server rule, it is possible that the defendant would get his way (if the server were in California) while the Irish woman would be disadvantaged, both by having to travel to California and by the application of a law far less amenable to defamation claims. And matters might be even worse if the website is hosted on a server that is in neither jurisdiction. Perhaps the website is hosted on a commercial server farm, the physical location of which is Nashville, Tennessee. In that situation, it would be absurd for courts in Tennessee to agree to hear the case since that state has no special interest in the outcome and the forum would be inconvenient for both parties.

For these reasons, and because it is more in accord with traditional practice around non-Internet cases, many courts will apply different reasoning to deciding the question of jurisdiction. They will often defer to the plaintiff's choice about where to bring the suit if there are any reasonable grounds to expect the defendant to defend itself in that jurisdiction. So they ask if there was deliberate intent to be involved in some way with the particular place where the court is located. In our defamation example, a Dublin court could well decide that the Californian defendant knew that the person about whom he said unflattering things lived in Dublin, so he was taking the chance of being sued in an Irish court and had no grounds to complain. Likewise, a business might have to defend itself in any number of jurisdictions if the courts felt that the business had substantial and intentional contacts with those areas. An online educational program, for instance, that advertised on Spanish-language websites and recruited some of its students from Mexico probably could not object to being forced into court in Mexico City. Indeed, the company Yahoo! was sued in a French court, under French laws, for selling Nazi memorabilia through its online site in which individuals could offer their own possessions for sale. The court found that Yahoo! had sufficient contacts through its various businesses to make it fair that Yahoo! be held to account in that country. The court then applied the French law against the sale of such memorabilia and ordered Yahoo! to stop making those items available to users of its sites on French soil (see Goldsmith and Wu 2006, 1–10).

Because the long reach of this principle[2] allows a lawsuit to go forward in any jurisdiction in which a defendant has had sufficient contacts so that it would not be manifestly unfair for that defendant to be expected to defend in those courts, many different courts may have jurisdiction over any specific complaint arising from online activity. So the online environment can be a very uncertain place, posing the risk of having to account for many different national laws when contemplating an Internet presence or online activity. This risk is mitigated somewhat, however, by international treaties that are intended to harmonize the copyright laws of many different nations.

---

2. In fact, the laws that implement this rule in the United States are often called "Long-Arm Statutes."

INTERNATIONAL TREATIES

The oldest international treaty on copyright that is still in force is the Berne Convention for the Protection of Literary and Artistic Works, which was first accepted by a group of nine signatories in 1886.[3] Since then it has been revised over half a dozen times, and there are now 165 nations that adhere to the Berne Convention, many of them because membership in the World Trade Organization now requires adherence to the Berne Convention.[4] The United States declined to join the Berne Convention for more than a hundred years because of the dramatic changes it would require in US law, finally signing on to the convention and partly implementing those changes in 1988. There are six aspects of the Berne Convention that will help us understand the international copyright landscape and the way national copyright laws apply to Internet activities.

The most important principle of the Berne Convention, at least in regard to deciding which law pertains to a particular activity, is the principle of *national treatment*, which tells members of Berne that they must apply the same copyright rules to citizens of any other member state that they would apply to their own citizens (see Berne Conv., art 5(1)). Thus, in Japan, my copyright in this book is protected by exactly the same rules as a copyright held by a Japanese citizen. And in the United States, a Japanese citizen has her copyright protected under the same US laws that protect mine. The advantage of this rule is that it tells all citizens of the Berne nations that they should observe the copyright laws of the nation where they live or are working, regardless of where the works involved had their origin.

In order that members not be disadvantaged by this rule of national treatment due to dramatic differences in national laws, the Berne Con-

---

3.   The current text of the Berne Convention can be found on the website of the World Intellectual Property Organization, the United Nations–sponsored organization that administers the treaty, at www.wipo.int/treaties/en/text.jsp?file_id=283698.

4.   Under the WTO's agreement on Trade-Related Aspects of Intellectual Property, or TRIPS.

vention stipulates *minimum standards* of protection for copyrights that each member nation is expected to enact in its own laws. The most significant of these minimum standards is that the term of copyright protection must be at least the life of the author plus fifty years in each Berne country (Berne Conv., art. 7 and 7bis). This requirement was a particular stumbling block for the United States when considering Berne membership, since our copyright law had always measured the term of protection by a set term of years. In the 1976 Copyright Act, that long-standing method of delimiting protection was changed in anticipation of joining the Berne Convention; the twenty-eight-year term, renewable once, was replaced by an absolute term of life of the author plus fifty years, which was later extended to life plus seventy years. Thus the US term of protection got much longer, and the way it was calculated was altered dramatically. As we will see, that change created some problems the United States had not previously encountered.

Another change that Berne membership necessitated for the Unite States was the *elimination of formalities* such as registration, notice (the © symbol that was previously required for copyright protection), and the need to renew a copyright after half of the term had expired. The Berne Convention requires that "the enjoyment and exercise" of the rights protected by the Convention "shall not be subject to any formality" (Berne Conv., art. 5(2)), so the United States had to repeal its renewal and notice requirements when it joined. Along with the change in term, this necessity, which makes copyright protection automatic and immediate for any work of original expression at the moment it is fixed in a tangible medium of expression, helps to create the significant "orphan work problem" that we have in the United States, which will be discussed shortly.

If these three important features of the Berne Convention brought about major changes in the copyright law of the United States and created some new problems for it to address, there are three other features of the treaty that, while significant, have not resulted in similar sweeping change, largely because the United States has not lived up to its promise to implement these features.

So-called *moral rights* are one of these features of Berne, and per-haps the one that gets the most attention. Most countries outside of the Anglo-American legal context provide a guarantee that the rights of an author or other creator to always have her name associated with her work and to not have the work altered in ways detrimental to her reputation will be protected. The Berne Convention obligates member nations to protect these moral rights of attribution and integrity (see Berne Conv., art 6bis). These rights are held, in most countries, by the creator or the creator's family, even after the "economic" rights have been transferred to a third party. The tradition of moral rights, however, developed out of a "natural rights" theory of copyright, which has always been antithetical to the Anglo-American focus on the economic rights as purely a creation of statutory law. So the United States has been reluctant to implement these moral rights into our national law, claiming that other parts of the law, particularly trademark and rules about false designation of origin, provide sufficient protection.

For scholars in the United States, this lack of protection for a right of attribution can be very problematic. For most academics, after all, the credit they receive for their work is the source of its primary value; reputation and impact on a field determine most of the rewards that aca-demic scholarship offers, such as promotion and tenure. Without some guarantee of continuous attribution, academic authors could be deprived of those rewards. Although it is certainly very rare, there are stories of works being published by a third-party rights holder, after transfer from the author, without the name of the author being credited. It is not clear that the current state of the law in the United States would provide a remedy for that situation.

The final two points about the requirements of the Berne conven-tion have less immediate impact on scholars than does the issue of attribution, and they can be handled quickly. First is the notion of the *rule of the shorter term*, which basically says that an author should not "normally" get any longer term of protection abroad than she would in her own country. In the United States, however, because we decided to "restore" copyright in foreign works for which the rights had lapsed because of the failure to follow the formalities that were in place up until 1989, some works are protected even after the copyright expires in the country of origin. The copyright in *Ulysses*, for example, has expired in the United Kingdom because seventy years have passed since James Joyce's death in 1941, but probably subsists in the United States under the restoration rules until 2018, which will be ninety-five years from its 1922 publication.[5]

The *three-step test* for copyright exceptions is the last part of the Berne Convention we will discuss, and one of the more controversial. As with moral rights and the rule of the shorter term, it is not clear how serious the United States is about complying with the three-step test, but overall uncertainties about its application make US doubts somewhat less conspicuous. The three-step test tells signatory nations that they may adopt whatever exceptions to copyrights that they see fit, provided that those exceptions apply to special cases, do not conflict with the normal exploitation of a work, and do not "unreasonably prejudice the legitimate interests of the author" (Berne Conv., art 9(2)). Because its language is so vague and subjective, there is considerable controversy over the application of the three-step test. From the perspective of scholars, the most troublesome possibility is that the US right of fair use, so indispensable to research and scholarly writing, might not meet this test. But there has never been an international challenge to fair use under the terms of Berne, and the fact that several other countries have become convinced of the value of a broad flexible exception like fair use[6] makes it very unlikely that the World Intellectual Property Organization (WIPO) would seriously consider such a challenge.

---

5. See 17 U.S.C. § 104A for a full description of the restored copyright in works of foreign origin.

6. The national legislatures of Israel and Japan, for example, both have adopted exceptions to their copyright laws based on fair use.

UNSETTLED QUESTIONS FOR THE BORDERLESS DIGITAL WORLD

With this background on the international copyright environment, we can now turn to two thorny and unresolved problems that bedevil the global scene. These are appropriate issues with which to finish our examination of IP for scholars because they help define the borders beyond which the questions of how intellectual property law and scholarship intersect in the digital world remain unsettled.

Orphan Works and Copyright Reform

There has been a great deal of discussion in the last decade over the so-called "orphan works problem." Orphan works are simply those books, movies, photographs, musical works, and so forth that are still protected by copyright but for which no rights holder can be located. The problem with orphan works is that copyright in such materials acts as a dead-weight loss economically. No productive use can be made of an orphan work without risking copyright infringement, yet there is no rights holder available from whom one can request permission for the use or to whom one can pay a licensing fee. Thus the copyright protection acts as a full stop on cultural advancement, which is precisely the opposite of the effect that copyright is intended to have.

What is seldom acknowledged about the orphan works problem is that, in the United States, it has been largely created by the decision to adhere, after over a century, to the Berne Convention.[7] Orphan works existed in the United States before we joined Berne, of course, but the size and scope of the problem grew exponentially because of changes in US law that were necessitated by Berne membership. Most notably, copyright became an "opt-out" rather than an "opt-in" system so that huge categories of material that would not have had a copyright under

7. For more detail on this point, see Smith 2012a, 2012c.

the older US law suddenly had full protection. When copyright became automatic at the moment of fixation, all manner of private papers, family photographs, home movies, and other materials suddenly had protection without the creators making any effort to seek that protection and even if they did not particularly want it. Furthermore, it became nearly impossible to opt out of that protection. Because the renewal requirement was abolished, there was literally no moment of decision at which a copyright holder could elect not to continue to lock up his or her work. Also, the term of copyright protection was extended dramatically to meet the standards imposed by Berne so that all works are, by definition, protected well past the death of their creators. This means that, even if the creators were aware of and desirous of the rights, which is not always or even often the case, those rights would inevitably pass to heirs, usually without any intentional bequest. Those heirs seldom realize that they hold those ancestral copyrights and make no efforts to exploit them or assist others to do so. Thus the Berne Convention creates huge swaths of intellectual property that then lies fallow for decades. Especially with photographs and films, many of these works may literally be reduced to dust before they can be used by the general public—a tragic and largely unnecessary cultural loss.

Awareness of the orphan works problem is worldwide, and many nations have considered or taken steps to address it. It is currently one of the major areas in which copyright reforms are being proposed. In the United States, Congress considered, but did not pass, the Shawn Bentley Orphan Works Act in 2008, which would have reduced the potential penalties for infringement that users might face if they had established, through a "reasonably diligent search" prior to the use, that the work was orphaned but were later confronted by an aggrieved rights holder.[8] In 2012, the US Copyright Office signaled that it was again interested in addressing the problem of orphan works when it issued a notice of inquiry asking various stakeholders, including the general public, to com-

---

8.   For details of this failed effort at reform, see GovTrack 2008.

ment on specific questions directed at mitigating that problem.[9] Although the new legislation has not yet been introduced, this renewed interest is notable because it has, for the first time, indicated that both one-time uses of individual works and large-scale mass digitization projects need to be addressed.

In other countries, several different kinds of orphan works solutions have been tried. In Canada and several other nations, there is a government board that is empowered to grant a license to users to make specific uses of orphan works once it has been established that no rights holder can be found through reasonable search efforts. Because this board always charges some licensing fee, even though that money seldom, if ever, actually benefits the rights holder, it has been successful in facilitating only a relatively few productive uses of orphan works.[10] In the European Union, the European Parliament adopted a directive in 2012 that instructs member countries to craft national laws to address the orphan works problem along specified lines.[11] One thing that is notable about the EU directive is that it specifically anticipates what it calls "trans-border uses" of orphan works, acknowledging that the Internet has created an intellectual property environment in which a patchwork of different, incompatible laws can lead to as many problems, and create as big an obstacle to productive use, as no laws at all.

The orphan works problem will almost certainly continue to receive a great deal of the attention that is directed toward copyright reform. It is especially important in the era when digital communications has facilitated all sorts of new distribution channels and encouraged mass digitization projects, mash-ups, and appropriation art, all of which cross international borders. As we have seen, a robust solution to this problem

9.   The notice of inquiry and all of the comments received are linked from the Copyright Office's website at www.copyright.gov/orphan.

10.   A detailed description of the law and an analysis of its impact is found in De Beer and Bouchard 2010.

11.   Details of the directive can be found on the website of the European Commission at http://ec.europa.eu/internal_market/copyright/orphan_works/index_en.htm.

might depend on a return to some kind of formalities like registration or renewal being required for the continuous and long-term enjoyment of copyright protection. Because such required formalities are forbidden under the current iteration of the Berne Convention, however, either that process will be very slow, or it will have to turn on voluntary measures.

First Sale in Analog and Digital

Another issue that has arisen at least partly because of the advent of digital communications technologies and that implicates international copyright law is the controversy over the doctrine of "first sale" in copyright. In 2012 the United States Supreme Court heard a case, called *Kirtsaeng v. John Wiley & Sons*, which had significant implications for copyright holders and users throughout the world.

Supap Kirtsaeng was a graduate student from Thailand. When he came to the United States to complete his education, he discovered that many of the textbooks that he and his fellow students had to buy cost significantly more in the United States than they did in Thailand. He conceived the idea of having his family purchase copies of these books in Thailand and selling them on the Internet, primarily to US students, for more than they cost abroad but less than the US retail price. His scheme was very successful and made a large profit until it was stopped by a lawsuit from a major textbook publisher. Such publishers depend on "price discrimination" to make their products attractive under different market conditions around the world, and John Wiley saw Kirtsaeng's business as a serious threat to that practice. In some ways, this story is about the potential of the Internet to flatten market conditions around the world.

Kirtsaeng lost his case at both the trial court and the appellate court level. In both instances, the courts held that the doctrine of first sale, which allows libraries to lend materials that have been lawfully obtained and allows consumers to resell the books, DVDs, and CDs that they purchase, actually applied only to copies of intellectual property that were manufactured in the United States. Works manufactured abroad, the courts said, were not "lawfully made under this title," which is the only condition the copyright law (Title 17 of the United States Code) places on this right to resell, rent, or lend materials without infringing the exclusive right of distribution. The Supreme Court agreed to review the case both because the Circuit Courts of Appeal are divided on the issue and because of the potential impact of the lower court ruling on activities as diverse as library lending, Internet services like Netflix, second-hand textbook opportunities for students, and consumer resale websites such as eBay.[12]

On March 19, 2013, the Supreme Court reversed the two lower courts' decisions in *Kirtsaeng v. Wiley*, holding that the doctrine of first sale was not limited by any geographical restriction. Instead, the court decided, any work of intellectual property that was made with the authorization of the rights holder—that is, one that is not a pirated copy—will be subject to the first sale exception to the exclusive right over distribution. Basically, if a work is entitled to copyright protection in the United States, it is also subject to all of the US limitations and exceptions. This decision was in accord with recent international developments as well; a European Union Copyright Directive recently instructed nations to recognize each members states' own version of first sale, called the doctrine of exhaustion in Europe, in all other member states.[13]

The decision in the *Kirtsaeng* case obviously is very important for scholars, both because it may have an impact on the textbook market, and therefore the cost of higher education, and because it assures the continued availability of the foreign works needed by scholars in their research. That is, it leaves in place the status quo for academic libraries, which can continue to purchase works from abroad, import them, and lend them to students and scholars for their research needs. It is also very likely that textbook publishers will move to Congress to try to readjust this situation through changes in the law now that a litigation strategy has failed.

12. The case is explained in SCOTUSblog 2013.
13. See Directive 2009/24/EC, of the European Parliament and of the Council of 23 April 2009 on the Legal Protection of Computer Programs, 2009 O.J. (L 111) 16.

On a greater level of generality, the conflict in *Kirtsaeng* points to a major development in the digital environment—the loss of the notion of ownership. First sale is predicated on the idea that once a consumer buys some work of intellectual property, he or she owns that particular copy and is free to further distribute it as he or she wishes. But in the digital environment, this whole notion of a particular copy that is transferred from the rights holder to a consumer, usually through the intermediation of a retail outlet, is upset. The sale of a digital asset does not involve a transfer of a single copy from a limited stock; it creates a new copy. Thus it is fairly clear that, regardless of the Supreme Court's decision in the *Kirtsaeng* case, the doctrine of first sale does not apply to digital works. The simple fact is that consumers do not own the e-books, MP3s, and digital movie files that they have purchased; they have merely licensed those works under contractual terms that allow the rights holder to retain ownership and control over the files and to cancel or modify the license at will. That basic situation was reinforced by a District Court decision in a different case that was handed down only days after *Kirtsaeng* that strongly rejected the expansion of first sale into the digital environment.[14]

This new environment in which licenses are replacing sales of intellectual property has already had some well-publicized effects. Customers of the Kindle e-book store run by Amazon had the experience of discovering that copies of the book *1984* by George Orwell that they thought they owned were suddenly removed from the readers by Amazon when the latter discovered it had not itself properly licensed the rights in the work.[15] More recently, there has been a lot of discussion about the ability of consumers who amass a large music collection in digital form to bequeath that collection when they die. The copyright law facilitated the inheritance of a large library of books or CDs, but under the regime of

---

14. The case was Capitol Records v. ReDigi in the Southern District of New York. For a news article about the case, see Albanese and Rosen 2013.

15. Newman 2009 details the controversy and lawsuit that developed from the removal of *1984*.

digital licenses, music and movie collections may now pass away at the same moment that the purchaser of them does.[16]

Although attention to the impact of licensing on digital intellectual property has largely focused on the situation for consumers generally, this dramatic change will have a significant impact specifically on scholars as well. The ability to incorporate third-party material into new works of scholarship could soon depend more on the terms of individual contracts than it will on the doctrine of fair use. E-books and online articles could even impose limitations on the length of quotations in new works, either through licensing limitations or by technological limits on the ability to "cut and paste." And it is certain, in any case, that the ability to access the materials needed on which to build new scholarship will be determined as much or more by licenses, in the foreseeable future anyway, than it is by copyright law.

The digital environment offers a great many advantages for scholarship, including better access to more of the building blocks of creativity and the ability to interact with other scholars around the world. The advantages certainly outweigh the risks, especially if scholars are able to manage the terms of distribution and access themselves rather than surrendering that control to commercial interests. But the changes wrought by digital technologies and by the new awareness of the trans-border environment in which intellectual property operates will not automatically favor scholarship and scholars. It will be necessary to pay much closer attention than ever before to national legislation in the area of copyright, to international treaties and negotiations, and to the licenses for digital access that are now becoming so ubiquitous.

---

16. A nice explanation of this dilemma is found in Mataconis 2012.

CONCLUSION

The world in which scholarship takes place today is very different from that in which St. Columba or Galileo did his work. But like them, scholars today must adapt to rapidly changing conditions. Intellectual property laws offer both some sense of continuity and the challenge of rapid change. For better or for worse, it is no longer possible to ignore the environment created by those laws or to assume that scholarly pursuits will always be allowed in precisely the way we would like to proceed. The price of the faster, more collaborative scholarly practices that are now possible is the need to be aware of the current IP environment for scholarship and attentive to the inevitable changes in that environment. Hopefully, this book can help to foster that awareness, even though some of its specific points will be superseded in the rapidly changing world of intellectual property and scholarship.

Works Cited

"About *Vectors*." 2014. Accessed July 21. http://vectors.usc.edu/journal/index. php?page=Introduction.

Albanese, Andrew, and Judith Rosen. 2013. "In ReDigi Case, Court Forcefully Rejects Digital First Sale." *Publishers Weekly*, April 2. www.publishersweekly.com/pw/ by-topic/digital/copyright/article/56632-in-redigi-case-court-rejects-digital-first-sale.html.

ARL (Association of Research Libraries). 2012. *Code of Best Practices in Fair Use for Academic and Research Libraries*. Washington, DC: Association of Research Libraries. www.arl.org/storage/documents/publications/code-of-best-practices-fair-use.pdf.

Aufderheide, Patricia. "MediaPro Also Uses Fair Use Best Practices Statement for Insurance Policies." *Fair Use* (blog), CMSI, February 24. www.cmsimpact.org/ blog/fair-use/mediapro-also-uses-fair-use-best-practices-statement-insurance-policies.

Ballon, Hilary, and Mariet Westermann. 2006. *Art History and Its Publications in the Electronic Age*. Houston: Rice University Press.

Barbrook, Richard. 2007. *Imaginary Futures: From Thinking Machines to the Global Village*. London: Pluto.

Barnet, Darin. 2004. *The Network Society*. Malden MA: Polity Press.

Benkler, Yochai. 2006. *The Wealth of Networks: How Social Production Transforms Markets and Freedom*. New Haven, CT: Yale University Press.

"Berlin Declaration on Open Access to Knowledge in the Sciences and Humanities." 2003. October 22. http://openaccess.mpg.de/286432/Berlin-Declaration.

Berne Convention for the Protection of Literary and Artistic Works. 1971. Adopted September 9, 1886; completed May 4, 1896; revised November 13, 1908; completed March 20, 1914; revised June 2, 1928; revised June 26, 1948; revised July 14, 1967; revised July 24, 1971. Available at www.law.cornell.edu/treaties/berne/overview.html.

Berne Convention for the Protection of Literary and Artistic Works. 1979. Adopted September 9, 1886; completed May 4, 1896; revised November 13, 1908; completed March 20, 1914; revised June 2, 1928; revised June 26, 1948; revised July 14, 1967; revised July 24, 1971; amended September 28, 1979. Available at www.wipo.int/treaties/en/text.jsp?file_id=283698.

"Bethesda Statement on Open Access Publishing." 2003. June 20. http://legacy.earlham.edu/~peters/fos/bethesda.htm.

Bielstein, Susan M. 2006. *Permissions, A Survival Guide: Blunt Talk about Art as Intellectual Property*. Chicago: University of Chicago Press.

Blumenstyk, Goldie. 2003. "Inventions Produced Almost $1 Billion for Universities in 2002." *Chronicle of Higher Education*, 19 December, A28.

BMC (BioMed Central). 2014. *BMC Medicine* website. Accessed July 21. www.biomedcentral.com/bmcmed.

BOAI (Budapest Open Access Initiative). 2002. February 14. www.budapestopenaccessinitiative.org/read.

Bosch, Stephen, and Kittie Henderson. 2013. "Winds of Change: Periodicals Price Survey 2013." *Library Journal,* April 25, 2013. http://lj.libraryjournal.com/2013/04/publishing/the-winds-of-change-periodicals-price-survey-2013.

Bosch, Stephen, Kittie Henderson, and Heather Klusendorf. 2011. "Periodicals Price Survey 2011: Under Pressure, Times Are Changing." *Library Journal*, April 1. http://lj.libraryjournal.com/2011/04/publishing/periodicals-price-survey-2011-under-pressure-times-are-changing.

Boswell, James. 1925. *The Life of Samuel Johnson*, vol. 2. Edited and with notes by Roger Ingpen. Bath, UK: George Bayntun. First published 1776.

Boyle, James. 2008. *The Public Domain: Enclosing the Commons of the Mind*. New Haven, CT: Yale University Press. Available for download at www.thepublicdomain.org.

Brand, Stewart. 1999. *The Clock of the Long Now: Time and Responsibility*. New York: Basic Books.

Brown, Patrick O., Diane Cabell, Aravinda Chakravarti, Barbara Cohen, Tony Delamothe, Michael Eisen, Les Grivell, et al. 2003. "Bethesda Statement on Open Access Publishing." June 20. http://legacy.earlham.edu/~peters/fos/bethesda.htm.

Butler, Alban. 1956. *Butler's Lives of the Saints*. Edited, revised, and supplemented by Herbert J. Thurston and Donald Attwater. Vol. 2, April, May, June. New York: P. J. Kennedy and Sons. First published 1756–59.

Capon, Robert Farrar. 2000. *The Fingerprints of God: Tracking the Divine Suspect through a History of Images*. Grand Rapids, MI: Wm. B. Eerdmans.

CIS (Center for Internet and Society). 2014. "Shloss v. Estate of Joyce." Stanford Law School. Accessed July 21. http://cyberlaw.stanford.edu/our-work/cases/shloss-v-estate-joyce.

"Cost of Knowledge" website. 2014. Accessed July 21. http://thecostofknowledge.com.

Crasson, Sara. 2004. "Are DeCSS T-Shirts Dirty Laundry? Wearable, Non-Executable Computer Code as Protected Speech." *Fordham Intellectual Property, Media and Entertainment Law* 15, no. 1: 169–201.

Crawford, Walt. 2011. *Open Access: What You Need to Know Now*. Chicago: ALA Editions

Creative Commons. 2009. *Defining "Noncommercial": A Study of How the Online Population Understands "Noncommercial Use."* San Francisco: Creative Commons, September. Available at http://wiki.creativecommons.org/Defining_Noncommercial.

Creative Commons. 2014a. "About CC0—'No Rights Reserved.'" Accessed July 22. http://creativecommons.org/about/cc0.

Creative Commons. 2014b. "About the Licenses." Accessed July 29. http://creativecommons.org/licenses.

"Crooked Timber." 2014. *Wikipedia*, last modified May 13. http://en.wikipedia.org/wiki/Crooked_Timber.

Dallmeier-Tiessen, Suenje, et al. 2011. "Highlights from the SOAP Project Survey: What Scientists Think about Open Access Publishing." arXiv:1101.5260, January 20. http://arxiv.org/ftp/arxiv/papers/1101/1101.5260.pdf.

Davis, Philip M. 2011. "Open Access, Readership, Citations: A Randomized Controlled Trial of Scientific Journal Publishing." *FASEB Journal* 25, no. 7 (July): 2129–34. doi:10.1096/fj.11-183988.

De Beer, Jeremy, and Mario Bouchard. 2010. "Canada's 'Orphan Works' Regime: Unlocatable Owners and the Copyright Board." *Oxford University Commonwealth Law Journal* 10, no. 2 (Winter). http://papers.ssrn.com/sol3/papers.cfm?abstract_id=1916840.

Decherney, Peter. 2012. *Hollywood's Copyright Wars: From Edison to the Internet*. New York: Columbia University Press.

"DeCSS." 2014. *Wikipedia*, last modified April 20. http://en.wikipedia.org/wiki/DeCSS.

Dreyfuss, Rochelle Cooper. 1987. "The Creative Employee and the Copyright Act of 1976." *University of Chicago Law Review* 56 (1987): 590–647.

Dreyfuss, Rochelle Cooper, and Roberta Rosenthal Kwall. 1996. *Intellectual Property* New York: Foundation Press.

Duke Law. 2010. "About Us." Center for the Study of the Public Domain. Accessed December 28. www.law.duke.edu/cspd/about.html.

Duke University. 2008. "Policy on Inventions, Patents, and Technology Transfer." *Faculty Handbook*, P-7–P12. https://olv.duke.edu/assets/docs/policy_on_inventions.pdf.

Duke University. 2014. "Avoiding Plagiarism." Accessed July 21. http://library.duke.edu/research/plagiarism.

Falcon, Joseph. 2009. "Do You Own 'Shop Right' in Your Employee's Invention?" *Pennsylvania Litigation* (blog), October. www.palitigationblog.com/2009/10/articles/intellectual-property-disputes/do-you-own-shop-right-to-your-employees-invention (site discontinued).

Ferreri, Eric. 2013. "A High-Tech Look at Ancient Civilizations." Duke Today, March 29, http://today.duke.edu/2013/03/maurizioforte.

Fitzpatrick, Kathleen. 2011. *Planned Obsolescence: Publishing, Technology and the Future of the Academy.* New York: New York University Press.

Forte, Maurizio. 2000. *Virtual Reality in Archaeology.* Oxford: Archaeopress.

Foster, Frank, and Robert Shook. 1993. *Patents, Copyright and Trademarks.* New York: John Wiley & Sons.

Fowler, Kristine K. 2012. "Do Mathematicians Get the Authors Rights They Want?" Scripta Manent, *Notices of the American Mathematical Society* 59, no. 3 (March): 436–38. www.ams.org/notices/201203/rtx120300436p.pdf.

Friedman, Thomas. 2005. *The World Is Flat: A Brief History of the Twenty-First Century.* New York: Farrar, Straus and Giroux.

Gargouri, Yassine, Chawki Hajjem, Vincent Larivière, Yves Gingras, Les Carr, Tim Brody, and Stevan Harnad. 2010. "Self-Selected or Mandated, Open Access Increases Citation Impact for Higher Quality Research." *PLOS ONE* 5, no. 10 (October 18): e13636. doi:10.1371/journal.pone.0013636.

Goldberg, David Theo, and Stefka Hristova. 2014. "Blue Velvet: Re-dressing New Orleans in Katwrina's Wake." Accessed August 8. http://vectors.usc.edu/projects/index.php?project=82.

Goldsmith, Jack, and Tim Wu. 2006. *Who Controls the Internet? Illusions of a Borderless World.* New York: Oxford University Press.

GovTrack. 2008. "S. 2913 (110th): Shawn Bentley Orphan Works Act of 2008." https://www.govtrack.us/congress/bills/110/s2913.

Guthrie, Kevin M. 2007. Preface to *University Publishing in a Digital Age,* by Laura Brown, Rebecca Griffiths, and Matthew Rascoff. New York: Ithaka. Available at http://scholarlypublishing.org/ithakareport/archives/7.

Hagerty, Barbara Bradley. 2009. *The Fingerprints of God: The Search for the Science of Spirituality.* New York: Riverhead Books.

Hall, Marie Boas. 2002. *Henry Oldenburg: Shaping the Royal Society.* New York: Oxford University Press.

Halperin, Mark. 2007. "A Great Idea Lives Forever. Shouldn't Its Copyright?" *New York Times,* May 20. www.nytimes.com/2007/05/20/opinion/20helprin.html.

Halperin, Mark. 2009. *Digital Barbarism: A Writer's Manifesto.* New York: Harper.

Hartman, Peri, Jeffrey P. Bezos, Shel Kaphan, and Joel Spiegel. 1999. "Method and System for Placing a Purchase Order via a Communications Network." US Patent 5,960,411, filed September 12, 1997, and issued September 28, 1999.

Hawes, Gene R. 1967. *To Advance Knowledge: A Handbook on American University Press Publishing.* Washington, DC: American University Press Services.

Hirtle, Peter. 2008. "Copyright Renewal, Copyright Restoration, and the Difficulty of Determining Copyright Status." *D-Lib Magazine* 14, no. 7/8 (July/August). www.dlib.org/dlib/july08/hirtle/07hirtle.html.

Hirtle, Peter. 2014. "Copyright Term and the Public Domain in the United States," January 1. https://copyright.cornell.edu/resources/publicdomain.cfm.

Hitchcock, Steve. 2013. "The Effect of Open Access and Downloads ('Hits') on Citation Impact: A Bibliography of Studies." Open Citation Project, last updated June 25. http://opcit.eprints.org/oacitation-biblio.html.

Houghton, Sarah. 2010. "Music in Libraries: We're Doing It Wrong." *Librarian in Black* (blog), September 6. http://librarianinblack.net/librarianinblack/2010/09/music-in-libraries-were-doing-it-wrong.html.

Intellectual Property Office. 2014. "New Exceptions to Copyright Reflect Digital Age." News release, June 1. https://www.gov.uk/government/news/new-exceptions-to-copyright-reflect-digital-age.

IPO (Intellectual Property Owners Association). 2009. *Top 300 Organizations Granted U.S. Patents in 2009.* Washington, DC: Intellectual Property Owners Association. www.ipo.org/wp-content/uploads/2013/03/2009top300.pdf.

Johnson, Peter. 1996. "Pornography Drives Technology: Why Not to Censor the Internet." *Federal Communications Law Journal* 49, no. 1: 217–226.

Kasunic, Robert. 2008. "Is That All There Is? Reflections on the Nature of the Second Fair Use Factor." *Columbia Journal of Law and the Arts* 31, no. 4 (Summer): 101–41.

Kolowich, Steve. 2009. "A Call for Copyright Rebellion." Inside Higher Ed, November 6. www.insidehighered.com/news/2009/11/06/lessig.

Landes, William M., and Richard A. Posner. 2003. *The Economic Structure of Intellectual Property Law*. Cambridge, MA: Belknap Press.

Lange, David. 1981. "Recognizing the Public Domain." *Law and Contemporary Problems* 44, no. 4 (Autumn): 147–78.

Laurent, Olivier. 2010. "AFP v. Morel: The debate rages on." *British Journal of Photography Blog*, September 27. Accessed January 6, 2011. http://www.bjp-online.com/2010/09/afp-v-morel-the-debate-rages-on/.

Lederman, Doug. 2010. "Tweaking Technology Transfer." *Inside Higher Education*, October 5. www.insidehighered.com/news/2010/10/05/techtransfer.

Litman, Jessica. 2001. *Digital Copyright*. New York: Prometheus Books.

MacCallum, Catriona J. 2007. "When Is Open Access Not Open Access?" *PLOS Biology* 5, no. 10 (October 16): e285. doi:10.1371/journal.pbio.0050285.

Mataconis, Doug. 2012. "Who Owns Your iTunes Library When You Die?" *Outside the Beltway* (blog), September 3. www.outsidethebeltway.com/who-owns-your-itunes-library-when-you-die.

Maxwell, Elliot. 2012. *The Future of Taxpayer-Funded Research: Who Will Control Access to the Results?* Washington, DC: Committee for Economic Development.

McCullagh, Declan, and Donna Tam. 2012. "Instagram Apologizes to Users: We Won't Sell Your Photos." CNET, December 18. http://news.cnet.com/8301-1023_3-57559890-93/instagram-apologizes-to-users-we-wont-sell-your-photos.

McJohn, Stephen M. 2003. *Intellectual Property: Examples and Explanations*. New York: Aspen.

McSherry, Corynne. 2001. *Who Owns Academic Work? Battling for Control of Intellectual Property*. Cambridge, MA: Harvard University Press.

Medlen, Virginia Shaw. 1996. *Intellectual Property Protection: A Guide for Engineers*. Belmont, CA: Professional Publications.

Minzesheimer, Bob. 2011. "Librarians Launch Boycott in Battle over E-books." *USA Today*, March 8. http://usatoday30.usatoday.com/life/books/news/2011-03-08-libraries08_ST_N.htm.

MLA (Modern Language Association). 2006. *Report of the MLA Task Force on Evaluating Scholarship for Tenure and Promotion*. New York: Modern Language Association.

Moretti, Franco. 2005. *Maps, Graphs, Trees: Abstract Models for a Literary History*. New York: Verso.

NCSU (North Carolina State University). 2011. "TEACH Act Toolkit." Accessed February 15. www.provost.ncsu.edu/copyright/toolkit.

Netflix. 2014. "Netflix Terms of Use." Accessed July 21. https://www.netflix.com/TermsOfUse?locale=en-US.

Newman, Jared. 2009. "Amazon Settles Kindle '1984' Lawsuit." *PCWorld*, October 1. www.pcworld.com/article/172953/amazon_kindle_1984_lawsuit.html.

NIH (National Institutes of Health). 2014. "Public Access Policy." Last updated March 18. http://publicaccess.nih.gov.

NPG (Nature Publishing Group). 2012. "NPG Author License Policy." Accessed May. www.nature.com/authors/policies/license.html.

OAD (Open Access Directory). 2012. "Author Addenda." OAD Wiki, last updated October 15. http://oad.simmons.edu/oadwiki/Author_addenda.

OAD (Open Access Directory). 2013. "Publisher Policies on NIH-Funded Authors." OAD Wiki, last updated November 21. http://oad.simmons.edu/oadwiki/Publisher_policies_on_NIH-funded_authors.

O'Donnell, James J. 1998. *Avatars of the Word: From Papyrus to Cyberspace.* Cambridge, MA: Harvard University Press.

Packard, Ashley. 2002. "Copyright or Copy Wrong: An Analysis of University Claims to Faculty Works." *Communication Law and Policy* 7: 275–315.

Palfrey, John G. 2008. *Born Digital: Understanding the First Generation of Digital Natives* New York: Basic Books.

Patry, William. 2009. *Moral Panics and the Copyright Wars.* New York: Oxford University Press.

Patterson, Lyman Ray. 1968. *Copyright in Historical Perspective.* Nashville, TN: Vanderbilt University Press.

PCG (Publishers Communication Group). 2011. Journal Subscriptions Renewal Trends 2006–2011. Cambridge, MA: PCG. www.pcgplus.com/wp-content/uploads/2013/03/Journal-Subscription-Renewal-Trends.pdf.

Peoples, Lee F. 2009. "The Citation of Blogs in Judicial Opinions." *Tulane Journal of Technology and Intellectual Property* 13 (October 27). Available at the Social Science Research Network (SSRN), last revised April 17, 2011. http://ssrn.com/abstract=1495181.

PLOS (Public Library of Science). 2014. "License." Accessed July 22. www.plos.org/open-access/license.

"*PLOS ONE*." 2014. *Wikipedia*, last modified June 4. http://en.wikipedia.org/wiki/PLoS_ONE.

Pollock, Rufus. 2009. "Forever Minus a Day? Calculating Optimal Copyright Term." *Review of Economic Research on Copyright Issues* 6, no. 1: 35–60.

Priem, Jason, and Bradley M. Hemminger. 2012. "Decoupling the Scholarly Journal." In "Beyond Open Access: Visions for Open Evaluation of Scientific Papers by Post-publication Peer Review," ed. Nikolaus Kriegeskorte and Diana Deca, special issue, *Frontiers in Computational Neuroscience* 6, no. 19, doi:10.3389/fncom.2012.00019.

Priem, Jason, Dario Taraborelli, Paul Groth, and Cameron Neylon. 2011. "Alt Metrics: A Manifesto," v 1.01, September 28. http://altmetrics.org/manifesto.

Read, Brock. 2009. "Twitter Film Festival Goes Live at Duke U." *Chronicle of Higher Education*, April 15. http://chronicle.com/blogPost/Twitter-Film-Festival-Goes/4630.

Rehmeyer, Julie. 2009. "Mathematics by Collaboration." Science News, December 8. https://www.sciencenews.org/article/mathematics-collaboration.

Rich, Motoko. 2009. "Legal Battles over E-Book Rights to Older Works." *New York Times*, December 12. www.nytimes.com/2009/12/13/business/media/13ebooks.html.

Rose, Mark. 1993. *Authors and Owners: The Invention of Copyright.* Cambridge, MA: Harvard University Press.

Rowland, Fytton. 2002. "The Peer-Review Process." *Learned Publishing* 15, no. 4 (October): 247–58.

SCOTUSblog. 2013. "Kirtsaeng v. John Wiley & Sons, Inc." www.scotusblog.com/case-files/cases/kirtsaeng-v-john-wiley-sons-inc.

SHERPA/RoMEO. 2014. "Statistics for the 1592 Publishers in the RoMEO Database." Accessed July 21. www.sherpa.ac.uk/romeo/statistics.php.

Shieber, Stuart. 2009. "What Percentage of Open-Access Journals Charge Publication Fees?" *The Occasional Pamphlet* (blog), May 29. https://blogs.law.harvard.edu/pamphlet/2009/05/29/what-percentage-of-open-access-journals-charge-publication-fees.

Simon, Todd F. 1982–83. "Faculty Writings: Are They 'Works Made for Hire' under the 1976 Copyright Act?" *Journal of College and University Law* 9: 485–509.

Smith, Kevin. 2006. "Digital Rights Management." *Scholarly Communications @ Duke* (blog), December 26. http://blogs.library.duke.edu/scholcomm/2006/12/26/digital-rights-management-drm.

Smith, Kevin. 2010. "Reading the Fine Print." *Scholarly Communications @ Duke* (blog), July 27. http://blogs.library.duke.edu/scholcomm/2010/07/27/reading-the-fine-print.

Smith, Kevin. 2012a. "How to Solve the Berne Problem, Part 1." *Scholarly Communications @ Duke* (blog), April 18. http://blogs.library.duke.edu/scholcomm/2012/04/18/how-to-solve-the-berne-problem-part-1.

Smith, Kevin. 2012b. "Is the CCC Having an 'Instagram' Moment?" *Scholarly Communications @ Duke* (blog), December 20. http://blogs.library.duke.edu/ scholcomm/2012/12/20/is-the-ccc-having-an-instagram-moment.

Smith, Kevin. 2012c. "Keeping It Simple, or How to Solve the Berne Problem, Part 2." *Scholarly Communications @ Duke* (blog), April 20. http://blogs.library.duke.edu/ scholcomm/2012/04/20/keeping-it-simple-or-how-to-solve-the-berne-problem-part-2.

SPARC. 2007. "SPARC Author Addendum to Publication Agreement." www.sparc.arl. org/resources/authors/addendum-2007

Springer. 2012. "Springer Permits Commercial Use for Its Hybrid Open Access Program." News release, January 18. www.springer.com/about+springer/media/pr essreleases?SGWID=0-11002-6-1332921-0.

Stebbins, Michael. 2013. "Expanding Public Access to the Results of Federally Funded Research." *Office of Science and Technology Policy* (blog), February 22. www. whitehouse.gov/blog/2013/02/22/expanding-public-access-results-federally-funded-research.

Stiglitz, Joseph. 1999. "Knowledge as a Global Public Good." In *Global Public Goods: International Cooperation in the 21st Century,* edited by Inge Kaul, Isabelle Grunberg, and Marc Stern, 308–25. New York: Oxford University Press.

Suber, Peter. 2008 "Gratis and Libre Open Access." *SPARC Open Access Newsletter,* August 2. www.sparc.arl.org/resource/gratis-and-libre-open-access.

Suber, Peter. 2012. *Open Access.* Cambridge, MA: MIT Press. http://bit.ly/oa-book.

Sunstein, Cass. 2007. *Republic.com 2.0.* Princeton, NJ: Princeton University Press.

Swan, Alma. 2012. *Policy Guidelines for the Development and Promotion of Open Access,* Paris: UNESCO, unesdoc.unesco.org/images/0021/002158/215863e.pdf.

Talbot, C. H. 1958. "The Universities and the Medieval Library." In *The English Library before 1700: Studies in Its History,* edited by Francis Wormald, 66–84. London: University of London, Athlone Press.

"Thanatos4." 2006. "Collaborative Digital Brain Mapping Comes of Age." Physics Forums, March 19, www.physicsforums.com/showthread.php?t=114840.

Thompson, John B. 2005. *Books in the Digital Age.* Cambridge: Polity Press.

Turow, Scott. 2013. "The Slow Death of the American Author." *New York Times,* April 7. www.nytimes.com/2013/04/08/opinion/the-slow-death-of-the-american-author.html.

University of Texas. 2014a. "FOB: Firms Out of Business." Harry Ransom Center, University of Texas at Austin, accessed July 21, 2014. http://norman.hrc.utexas. edu/watch/fob.cfm.

University of Texas. 2014b. "WATCH: Writers Artists and Their Copyright Holders."
    Harry Ransom Center, University of Texas at Austin, accessed July 21, 2014.
    http://norman.hrc.utexas.edu/watch.

US Patent and Trademark Office. 2014. "Fee Schedule." Last updated May 12. www.
    uspto.gov/web/offices/ac/qs/ope/fee010114.htm.

Vaidhyanathan, Siva. 2011. *The Googlization of Everything (and Why We Should
    Worry)*. Oakland: University of California Press.

Winston, Elizabeth I. 2006. "Why Sell What You Can License? Contracting around
    Statutory Protection of Intellectual Property." *George Mason Law Review* 14, no. 1
    (Fall): 93–133.

Wooten, David. 2010. *Galileo: Watcher of the Skies*. New Haven, CT: Yale University
    Press.

Zhang, Yanjun. 2006. "The Effect of Open Access on Citation Impact: A Comparison
    Study Based on Web Citation Analysis." *Libri* 56, no. 3: 145–54.

Index